ABOUT THIS BOOK

The purpose of this book is to show that many SanJuanist commentators err in portraying St. John of the Cross only as a world-negating contemplative and by misunderstanding him only as the "Doctor of the Dark Night of the Soul." This misinterpretation is informed by a failure to understand John's historical context, including the problem of *conversos* in sixteenth century Spain, as well as by a failure to understand his multi-faceted life.

The originality of this book lies in its close examination of John's life and writings by using Raimundo Panikkar's tripartite model of salvation, namely the mystical paths of action (*karma yoga*), wisdom (*jñâna yoga*), and devotion (*bhakti yoga*). Panikkar borrows that terminology from the Hindu tradition. Yet, he saw the important roles that action, wisdom, and devotion also play in the Christian mystical tradition. He associated the path of action with apostolic service, the path of wisdom with loving knowledge (in John's words "*noticia amorosa*"), and the path of devotion and love with affective mysticism.

It is time to study St. John of the Cross as a whole person, bringing together his multifaceted dimensions and his historical context. Attention should be devoted to his active role in the Carmelite tradition as a religious reformer, an administrator, and a prophet; to his intellectual capacity as a mystical theologian and teacher; to his religious devotion as a poet, friar, hermit, spiritual director, confessor, and priest; and to his Moorish and possibly also Jewish roots.

This book also presents a brief history of contemplation and action in the Christian mystical tradition, and then reviews contemplation and action in John's life and writings. In addition, as noted. it examines John's writings through Panikkar's tripartite model of action, wisdom, and devotion. Finally, it concludes with an assessment of the SanJuanist legacy for today's world, including his eco-spiritual significance.

ABOUT THE AUTHOR

CRISTÓBAL SERRÁN-PAGÁN y FUENTES is a native of Spain, like San Juan de la Cruz, and he has spent the last three decades in the United States doing research on Thomas Merton and St. John of the Cross. He received his Ph.D. in Religious Studies from Boston University. The title of his dissertation was, "Mystical Vision and Prophetic Voice in Saint John of the Cross: Towards a Mystical Theology of Final Integration."

He is currently an Associate Professor in the Department of Philosophy and Religious Studies at Valdosta State University in the State of Georgia. He is also a member of The International Thomas Merton Society, and has served for several years as an advisor to the Robert Daggy Scholarship Program. In addition, he is a regular contributor to Merton conferences in Europe and the United States.

Some of his publications on Thomas Merton and St. John of the Cross can be found in *Thomas Merton: A Mind Awake in the Dark* (Three Peaks Press, 2002), in *Seeds of Hope: Thomas Merton's Contemplative Message* (Cistercium-Ciem, 2008), and in *The Merton Annual* Volume 30 (Fons Vitae 2017). He is the also editor of the Fons Vitae volume on *Merton and the Tao*.

Further, he has taught summer courses in Spanish mysticism as part of the Madrid, Spain study-abroad program in El Colegio Mayor Padre Poveda. And, over many years he has taken faculty members, students, and conference retreatants on numerous field trips to visit SanJuanist sites, especially in Ávila, Salamanca, Segovia, Toledo, Álcala de Henares, Granada, Baeza, Úbeda, and La Carolina.

SAINT JOHN OF THE CROSS

HIS PROPHETIC MYSTICISM IN THE HISTORICAL CONTEXT OF SIXTEENTH-CENTURY SPAIN

Cristóbal Serrán-Pagán y Fuentes

PACEM IN TERRIS PRESS

Devoted to the global vision of Saint John XXIII,
prophetic founder of Postmodern Catholic Social Teaching,
and in support of the search for a Postmodern Ecological Civilization,
which will seek to learn from the rich spiritual wisdom-traditions
of Christianity and of our entire global human family.

www.paceminterrispress.com

2018

Copyright © 2018 Cristóbal Serrán-Pagán y Fuentes
All Rights Reserved

ISBN-13: 978-0999608876
ISBN-10: 0999608878

With gratitude to the Washington Province of the Discalced Carmelites ICS Publications for permission to reprint quotations from John of the Cross.

Cover photo from statue of Saint John of the Cross in Caravaca de la Cruz, Murcia, Spain, courtesy of the Caravaca Office of Tourism. The statue was completed in 1986 by the sculptor Rafael Pi Belda, in commemoration of the Fourth Centenary of the foundation of the Convento del Carmen. The style is neobaroque and manifests John's humanity.

Pacem in Terris Press publishes scholarly books directly or indirectly related to Catholic Social Teaching and its commitment to justice, peace, ecology, and spirituality, and on behalf of the search for a Postmodern Ecological Civilization.

In addition, in order to support ecumenical and interfaith dialogue, as well as dialogue with other spiritual seekers, Pacem in Terris Press publishes scholarly books from other Christian perspectives, from other religious perspectives, and from perspectives of other spiritual seekers that promote justice, peace, ecology, and spirituality for our global human family.

Opinions or claims expressed in publications from Pacem in Terris Press represent the opinions and claims of the authors and do not necessarily represent the official position of Pacem in Terris Press, the Pacem in Terris Ecological Initiative, Pax Romana / Catholic Movement for Intellectual & Cultural Affairs - USA or its officers, directors, members, and staff.

PACEM IN TERRIS PRESS
is the publishing service of

PAX ROMANA
Catholic Movement for Intellectual & Cultural Affairs
USA
*1025 Connecticut Avenue NW, Suite 1000,
Washington DC 20036
www.paceminterris.net*

TABLE OF CONTENTS

Preface by Joe Holland   1

Biographical Chronology   3

    Introduction   7

1. Contemplation & Action in the Christian Mystical Tradition   27

2. The Life & Writings of Saint John of the Cross   60

3. The Mystical Path of Action   95

4. The Mystical Path of Wisdom   114

5. The Mystical Path of Devotion   143

6. The SanJuanist Legacy for Today's World   156

Acknowledgments   173

Photos of Monuments of John of the Cross & Teresa of Avila   175

Bibliography   189

Other Books from Pacem in Terris Press   199

PREFACE

With this fascinating book, Dr. Cristóbal Serrán-Pagán y Fuentes gives us a rich and insightful study of the mystical vision and prophetic voice of great 16th Century Spanish Catholic Saint, John of the Cross. For this we are deeply in his debt. But rather than commenting in detail on this book which you will soon read for yourself, I would instead like to offer a few words about the book's author and his overall intellectual project.

The great academic loves of Dr. Serrán-Pagán y Fuentes are Theology and Philosophy. After graduating from Saint Thomas University in Miami Gardens, Florida, he went on to complete his Master of Arts in Philosophy at Boston College in Massachusetts. Next, he completed his Ph.D. in Religious Studies at Boston University.

Throughout his studies, he became fascinated by the phenomenon of mysticism in all world religions, and particularly its relationship to the prophetic spirit. Eventually, he devoted himself to the study of several Catholic mystical prophets.

The first was Thomas Merton. Merton had been an American bohemian mid-20th century intellectual and writer who had studied at Columbia University in New York City, and later surprisingly converted to Catholicism. He then became a Trappist monk and provided profound inspiration for Catholic participation in the dialogue with Buddhism, and also for the prophetic Catholic movement in the 1960's against the US war in Vietnam and more widely in Southeast Asia.

The second and third were Saint John of the Cross and Saint Teresa of Avila, in the the Spanish Carmelite tradition. He saw both as figures akin to Merton within their own historical-geographic context.

Thus, in this book, he accurately portrays John as holistically embracing the threefold mystical paths of action, wisdom, and love, and within the historical context of 16th-century *conversos* (converts) who were descendants of Jewish and Muslim families, all of whom were threatened by and often suffered from early-modern Spain's *pureza de sangre* (purity of blood) law.

In reading this fascinating book, you will learn why John, like his great and older mentor Teresa, was not an alienated mystic detached from the great issues of his time, but rather one immersed within them. In turn, he himself became a victim of the historical forces of religious oppression of his own time.

Saint John of the Cross has seldom been so profoundly presented, as you will find here in Dr. Serrán-Pagán y Fuentes' rich study which unveils the underlying unity of mysticism and prophecy in this great Spanish saint. We stand deeply in debt to the author for his pioneering and visionary study of this sainted figure who calls us to holistic engagement with the Divine Mystery, with the Cosmos, and with all of humanity through the unity of the mystical and the prophetic.

Joe Holland, Ph.D.
Emeritus Professor of Philosophy & Religion
Saint Thomas University, Miami Gardens, Florida, USA

BIOGRAPHICAL CHRONOLOGY

1515   On March 28, Teresa de Cepeda y Ahumada is born in Gotarrendura (Ávila). Her parents are Alonso Sánchez de Cepeda (from Toledo) and Beatriz de Ahumada (from Olmedo).

1522   Teresa leaves home with her brother Rodrigo to go to "the land of the Moors" in the heroic spirit of chivalry novels.

1528   Teresa's mother dies at Gotarrendura.

1531   Teresa's father sends her, with a reluctant spirit, to the Augustinian convent school of Santa María de Gracia.

1535   Teresa joins the Carmelite Convent of the Incarnation (Ávila).

1537   On November 3, Teresa professes as a Carmelite nun.

1538   Teresa stays at her sister's farm in Castellanos de la Cañada, where she reads Osuna's *Third Spiritual Alphabet*.

1539   She goes to Becedas to be treated by a female healer. On August 15, she collapses for three days and is prepared for burial. She remains an invalid for three years.

1542?   Juan de Yepes y Álvarez is born in Fontiveros (Ávila).

1544   On December 26, Teresa witnesses the death of her father, Alonso.

1545   Gonzalo, John's father, dies.

1551   Family moves to Medina del Campo where John attends the Catechism school (*en el Colegio de los Doctrinos*).

1554   Teresa experiences her first religious conversion in the presence of the suffering Christ.

1555   John studies humanities in a Jesuit college in Medina.

1562   In June, Teresa finishes her autobiographical book.

	On August 24, she founds her first reformed convent, St. Joseph's, in Ávila. She begins to write *The Way of Perfection*.
1563	Teresa writes the *Constitutions* of her reform, giving the name of "Discalced" or "Barefoot" Carmelites. John enters the novitiate of the "Calced" Carmelites at Santa Ana in Medina, calling himself John of Saint Matthias (Juan de Santo Matía).
1564	John is sent to study arts, theology, and philosophy at the University of Salamanca for four years.
1566	Teresa writes the first draft of *Meditations on the Song of Songs*.
1567	In July, John is ordained in Salamanca. He says his first Mass in Medina. He meets Teresa for the first time.
1568	John joins Teresa in the Carmelite reform, taking the name of John of the Cross (Juan de la Cruz). On November 28, he starts, with two other friars, the first Discalced house in Duruelo.
1569	Teresa writes her *Exclamations*.
1571	John travels with Teresa to Alba de Tormes. He becomes the rector of the Carmelite house of studies of Alcalá de Henares.
1572	John becomes the vicar and confessor at the Convent of the Incarnation in Ávila. Teresa writes the *Spiritual Challenge*. In January, Teresa sees herself being clothed with a gown of dazzling whiteness by the Virgin Mary.
1573	Teresa begins to write the *Foundations*.
1576	The Inquisition in Seville interrogates Teresa after a novice denounces her. John is imprisoned in Medina.
1577	John is abducted in Ávila and is put into prison in Toledo; he starts writing the *Spiritual Canticle*. Teresa begins to write the *Interior Castle*.
1578	In August, John escapes from prison and seeks refuge in Andalusia. He becomes the vicar of El Calvario (Jaén).
1579	John composes the "Sketch of the Mount." He establishes the Carmelite house of studies in Baeza. On June 6, Teresa writes her *Four Warnings*.

1580	John's mother, Catalina, dies in Medina. Teresa's brother, Lorenzo, dies. John visits Caravaca (Murcia) at Teresa's request. On June 22, Gregory XIII officially divides the Carmelite Order into the autonomous branches.
1581	John meets with Teresa for the last time and invites her to go to Granada with him, but she decides not to go.
1582	John becomes the prior of the Carmelite house of Los Mártires in Granada where he writes commentaries on his earlier poems. On October 4, St. Teresa dies in Alba de Tormes.
1585	In February, John travels to Málaga for the nun's foundation. In May, he travels to Lisbon. He becomes vicar of Andalusia.
1586	On May 18, John founds a convent in Córdoba.
1588	John becomes prior at Segovia. John is elected as officer in the governing body of the Discalced Carmelite Order.
1590	Nicholas Doria, the hermit of Pastrana, who advocated for strict observance and austerity, deprives John of his office.
1591	Doria wants to send John to Mexico, although John becomes ill and is sent to the hermitage of La Peñuela (Jaén). He dies on December 14 at midnight a lonely death, covered with sores.
1593	John's remains are transferred to Segovia (perhaps alluded to by Cervantes in *Don Quixote* 1, 19).
1614	Teresa is beatified by Paul V.
1622	On March 12, Gregory XV canonizes Teresa.
1675	On January 25, Clement X beatifies John.
1726	On December 27, Benedict XIII canonizes John.
1926	On August 24, Pious XI declares John Doctor of the Church.
1952	John is named the patron of the Spanish poets.
1970	On September 27, Paul VI declares Teresa Doctor of the Church.

INTRODUCTION

The purpose of this book is to show that many SanJuanist commentators err in portraying St. John of the Cross as a world-negating contemplative by calling him the doctor of the dark night of the soul.

This misinterpretation is informed by a failure to understand John's historical context (the problem of *conversos* in sixteenth century Spain) and his rich tradition of mystical theology, which John inherited from Pseudo-Dionysius through to medieval Christian mystics, and then most surely to Sufi mystics (Ibn Al'Arabi of Murcia and Ibn Abd of Ronda) and Jewish Kabbalistic mystics (Moses de León), who by then had left a great spiritual legacy in the Iberian Peninsula. For the Christian mystical tradition, in which the Carmelite saint was deeply immersed, the contemplative and the prophetic are two aspects of the same reality. Mary often symbolizes the contemplative mystic, while Martha best represents the active mystic.

This study sheds light on the essential role that St. John of the Cross played in the history of Christianity by acknowledging both the mystical and the prophetic dimensions of his life testimonies and writings. The notion of prophetic mysticism is not altogether foreign to the Carmelite tradition, especially when it follows the prophetic example of Elijah.

The originality of this book lies in a close examination of John's life and writings using Raimundo Panikkar's tripartite model of salvation, namely the mystical paths of action (*karma yoga*), wisdom (*jñâna yoga*), and devotion (*bhakti yoga*). Panikkar borrows the terminology from the Hindu tradition. He saw the important roles that action, wisdom, and devotion play in the Christian mystical tradition by associating the path of action with apostolic service, the path of wisdom with loving knowledge (in John's words "*noticia amorosa*"), and the path of devotion and love with affective mysticism.

It is time to study St. John of the Cross as a whole person, bringing together his historical context and multifaceted dimensions. Attention should be devoted to his active role in the Carmelite tradition as a religious reformer, an administrator, and a prophet; to his intellectual capacity as a mystical theologian and teacher; and to his religious devotion as a poet, friar, hermit, spiritual director, confessor, and priest.

The book presents a brief history of contemplation and action in the Christian mystical tradition and reviews the biography and writings of this Carmelite saint. Again, it examines John's writings through appeal to Raimundo Panikkar's tripartite model of action, wisdom, and devotion. Finally, it concludes with an assessment of the SanJuanist legacy for today's world.

St. John of the Cross (1542?-1591), the Doctor of *la Nada* (the No-thingness), is also the Doctor of *el Todo* (the All). The Carmelite saint has become an icon for the Catholic Church. Yet John is often portrayed by many commentators only as a model of sanctity reached only by practicing an austere, ascetic, contemplative life. Furthermore, many commentators understand John's active life only in the context of an apostolate of prayer. Even worse, some commentators are inclined to believe that John did not play an active role in his time.

For example, Bede Frost offers an odd argument for this view claiming that St. John of the Cross

> *played no part, humanly speaking, in that immense and stirring drama which filled the stage of sixteenth-century Europe. Nothing in his writings or in the slight contemporary references to him reveals the faintest interest in that interplay of vast political, economic, social and religious forces, so inextricably mingled, which strove together in that world writhing in the processes of disintegration and reformation. His*

> *portrait occupies no place in that gallery upon whose walls there hang the great men and women of the second half of the sixteenth century.*[1]

Thus, this Carmelite saint, widely known as a mystic, is not generally thought of as a reformer, even less a prophet. John the reformer is often characterized only as a pious monk whose

> *earnest desire was to strengthen the contemplative side of the constitutions. He feared lest the frequent coming and going, necessitated by sermons and conferences undertaken by the friars, should lead to relaxation of the solitude, prayer and penance essential to the Carmelite vocation ... He was also opposed to the undertaking of foreign missions. he considered that there were religious orders enough in the Church with that special end, whereas the Carmelite friars were intended, not to preach the gospel to pagan lands, but to promulgate its perfect practice in the home countries, by their example, their prayers, and their teaching.*[2]

In the words of researcher Peter Slattery:

> *St. Teresa worked hard with the support of the Prior General and other Church officials to spread the reform among the Carmelite order. St. John of the Cross took a less active role, but nevertheless earned the admiration of all as a faithful religious, renowned confessor and spiritual director ... Although St. John did not take much part in actively spreading the reform he was extremely influential as one of the founding friars, from*

---

[1] Bede Frost, *Saint John of the Cross. Doctor of Divine Love: An Introduction to His Philosophy, Theology and Spirituality* (London: Hodder & Stoughton, 1937), 1. The author of this book strongly believes that John's "silence and apparent lack of knowledge of and interest in contemporary history can hardly have been due to actual ignorance but had a far more fundamental source. From his early years he was drawn to a life of solitude, prayer and penance" (6). Frost claims that John's apparent lack of interest in the world was due to a long Christian practice of dying to the sins and to the things of the world. But Frost may well be incorrectly interpreting the monastic idea of *contemptus mundi*, even after studying John's life and thoughts.

[2] The Sisters of Notre Dame, *Life of Saint John of the Cross: Mystical Doctor* (New York: Benziger Brothers, 1927), 97-98.

> the character of his writings and poetry and his unquestioned sanctity. Others, like Fray Nicholas (Doria) and Fray Jerome (Gracian), took a more active role in the struggles of the early years of the reform. St. John was several times elected prior, definitor and consultor. Apart from some letters mostly dating from the last years of the saint's life, primary sources contemporary to events are scarce. At the chapter of 1591, St. John retired from all offices and wanted to live simply in Andalucia, his favorite place on earth.[3]

Another SanJuanist commentator makes the following observation:

> Unlike Teresa, he [John] was singularly devoid of all those vivid and arresting features that one calls personality. We see an inward looking, silent man with downcast eyes, hurrying off to hide himself in his cell and so absent-minded that he often did not take in what was said to him. We note the immense tenacity of purpose that underlay his somewhat feminine sensibility, his strictness in matters of discipline and his entire and whole-hearted devotion to the contemplative life.[4]

By contrast, I would argue that the Discalced Carmelite Order, cofounded by Teresa and John, affected not only the religious reforms of the sixteenth century but also the social fabric of the Castilian society, especially by providing a monastic refuge for women and *conversos* (both Jewish and Muslim converts).

Needless to say, women and *conversos* were the social groups that suffered the most during Philip II's reign as the monarch, and some of his delegates persecuted those who departed from the newly established codes for the Kingdom of Castile. Women and *conversos* were seen as potential threats to the new social and religious identity adopted by old Christians in the so-called reconquest of the Iberian Peninsula. Some of these *converso* women had strong ties to so-called heretical sects (*iluminadas* or

---

[3] Peter Slattery, *The Springs of Carmel: An Introduction to Carmelite Spirituality* (New York: Alba House, 1991), 70-71.

[4] Gerald Brenan, *St John of the Cross: His Life and Poetry* (Cambridge: Cambridge University Press, 1973), 83.

alumbradas). and they were seen as a threat to the new social and religious policies of the Spanish empire. In the meantime, Teresa and John opened their convents and monasteries to those women and *conversos* who did not have a place in the new society by accepting them in large numbers and by allowing them to play a significant role inside the Carmelite tradition.

Would it be possible, then, to say that John adopted the Discalced Carmelite Order, because he was a *converso* like Teresa and felt at home with her new proposed ideas for friars and nuns alike to be sheltered from the harsh times ("*tiempos recios*") of sixteenth century Castile? Certainly, it could very well be that John decided to join the Teresian reform because *conversos* were welcomed in the Discalced Carmelite Order until the end of the sixteenth century.

We know for sure that Teresa's father and grandfather had to carry out the infamous *sambenitos* through the streets of Toledo after declaring themselves to be penitent heretics for having practiced Judaism in secret. Also, it is well documented that the Teresian reform received financial support from *converso* families inside and outside the monastic walls.

Without doubt, John as coadjutor and administrator of the Discalced Carmelite Order, became well acquainted with Teresa's *converso* background and the large number of *conversos* within the Teresian reform. Coincidentally, John's father came from Yepes, a small town near Toledo where Teresa had also relatives. I wonder if their Jewish families knew each other already from those early days living in Yepes (Toledo).

What if the first meeting in Medina del Campo between Teresa and Juan had to do with being *conversos* from the province of Toledo where they have a network of family and friends who supported each other after Ferdinand and Isabella edicted in 1492 the laws of expulsion of Jews from the Iberian Peninsula.

Many Jews converted to the Catholic faith, knowing that this was the only solution for them to continue living in their homeland and preserve their private properties. Most people are unaware that Muslims were not forced to leave Spain until 1616 from the harbor of Valencia. We can only imagine why *conversos* would protect themselves and form a network of families that they associate themselves with through their lifetimes, because for them it was a matter of life and death under the new *pureza de sangre* (purity of blood) laws promulgated by old Christians and the inquisitors.

According to Serafín de Tapia, the Calced Carmelites adopted these purity of blood laws in 1566.[5] This new data supports my suspicion that the problem of *conversos* was at the heart of the major persecutions that both Teresa and John had to suffer at the hands of old Christians, including some of his Carmelite brothers.

What we can infer from all the new data available to us now is that most probably John's father came from a Jewish *converso* family, as Francisco Márquez Villanueva and José Gómez-Menor Fuentes have indicated in their research. In John's case we can only speculate because we don't have any documentation to prove or disprove his Jewish roots following his father's lineage.

However, as Asín Palacios, Pablo María Garrido, Lola Poveda, and Luce López Baralt have elucidated in their works, we can deduce that there is enough evidence to link John's *converso* lineage not only through his father's lineage as a *marrano,* which it is easier to prove in this case knowing that John's paternal family came from the *oficio of mercader de sedas* (the business of trading and selling silk products), but in the case of John's mother we know she came from the occupation of being a weaver, and this trade was typical of Muslim *conversos,* also known as *moriscas*.

Not only their families played well those societal roles, as did many other *converso* families, but more importantly John and Teresa always lived in towns and cities where there was a large *converso* population that serves

---

[5] Serafín de Tapia, "Las huellas y el legado de las tres culturas religiosas en Ávila". In *Vivencia Mística y Tejido Social* (Zamora: Ediciones Monte Casion, 2006) 206. According to this professor of history in the University of Salamanca, the Jewish *converso* population in Ávila was more than 20% and the Moorish *converso* population was between 10 and 15%. By 1570 many *moriscos* came from Granada seeking refuge after being dispersed in Las Alpujarras (210).

them well to protect themselves from the constant pressure exerted by old Christians and the holy inquisitors, whose major task was to make sure that the large Jewish and Muslim *converso* population in the kingdoms of Castile and Aragon will fully abide by the Christian laws and adopt the Roman Catholic faith without any hesitation or heretical deviation, as Teresa's family prove to have done in Toledo.

As a matter of fact, we know Teresa's family moved from Toledo to Ávila to escape from any suspicion in the eyes of the *Santo Oficio* (Holy Office). In so doing, her family, coming from a wealthy middle-class family of merchants, was able to purchase an old Christian last name from an *hidalgo* family. In those days it was a common practice among *converso* families to convert their old Jewish names into new Christian names; thereby, they were able to escape from any suspicion raised by old Christians living in their new adopted city of Ávila, where the Jewish and Muslim *converso* population was larger than other cities in Castile.

Could it be that the problem of *conversos* one of the main reasons why Teresa's and John's writings were denounced to the Holy Inquisition? In John's case, he was kidnapped twice by his own Calced Carmelite brothers and had to suffer persecutions until the end of his life, including Doria's effort to send John in exile to Mexico. But he ended up in Andalusia, where he received the mistreatment and abuse by his abbot in Úbeda.

In other words, the traditional narrative does not take into consideration this important historical factor of the two co-founders of the Discalced Carmelite tradition sharing *converso* lineages, at least through direct Jewish bloodline. As Daniel A. Dombrowski points out, in one of the most notable SanJuanist studies of the twentieth century:

> *No treatment of the social world of John of the Cross and Teresa of Avila would be adequate without the mention of the latter's Jewish roots. After the nobles and the higher clergy, the Jews had been the wealthiest and most influential people in Spain, a status which, when combined with anti-Semitism, led to the pogroms of the late fourteenth century and to the "reconciliation" of many Jews to Christianity in the Inquisition.*

> *Teresa of Avila's ancestors were among these. In fact, because her ancestros were, like John of the Cross's, Toledan silk merchants, there are reasons to suspect that John of the Cross may also have had Jewish roots.*[6]

Religious scholars tend to study the mystics' thoughts apart from their life events and historical circumstances. As Janet K. Ruffing observes:

> *Contemporary scholars in the field of mysticism often fail to take sufficiently into account the actual historical record, however, which might demonstrate that reforming mystics were engaged within their ecclesial bodies in a form of social transformation when they were concerned about mediating religious salvation to those who were marginalized within society, even when they did not address all of the other economic or social needs of the group they served. Sociologists, on the other hand, often fail to recognize the range of complex social processes related to the religion mystics practiced that contributed to and supported innovating or reforming movements (Coleman 1997 qtd. in Ruffing).*[7]

Many SanJuanist commentators, especially hagiographers, have been interested in giving the Carmelite saint a rigid, austere, pious image. They have ignored altogether John's involvement in the world. F.C Happold states the following on John's ambivalent portraits:

> *To some this gentle little Carmelite saint, as he has been called, the devoted companion of St Teresa, is utterly repellent. Of him one writer uses these words: 'terrible, sanglant et les yeux secs'; another labels him 'l'áscète terrible'. Yet others find him the most attractive of the contemplative saints. Why are there these apparently conflicting responses? The answer is not far to seek. St John of the Cross has two faces: he is both the apostle of absolute detachment and also the apostle of absolute love. He teaches a detachment so absolute that it appears, taken*

---

[6] Daniel A. Dombrowski, *St. John of the Cross: An Appreciation* (New York: State University of New York Press, 1992) 38.

[7] Janet K. Ruffing, "Ignatian Mysticism of Service," in *Mysticism & Social Transformation*, ed. Janet K. Ruffing (Syracuse, New York: Syracuse University Press, 2001), 107.

alone, to be a complete abandonment of everything earthly, a philosophy of world-negation of a most extreme type. But he can also write such sentences as: 'All the ability of my soul and body is moved through love, all that I do I do through love, and all that I suffer I suffer for love's sake,' and, in one of his letters: 'Where there is no love, put love in and you will draw love out.' And these two elements are intimately intertwined; the detachment is absolute because the love is absolute.[8]

The purpose of this study is to show that many SanJuanist commentators err in portraying John as a world-negating contemplative. This misinterpretation is informed by their failure to understand the true nature of the contemplative life. For John, contemplation does not mean complete withdrawal from the world or total absorption. Rather, the Carmelite saint includes in his broad definition of contemplation both the active life and the contemplative life (also known by Thomists as the mixed life).

In the Christian mystical tradition, Martha and Mary are sisters. They go hand in hand. Studying the Bible and the Christian tradition was a precondition for opening new Carmelite houses of study in the Teresian reform. At last, the mind and the heart are brought together in deep contemplation. As a result of achieving this "final integration," the founding fathers of the Discalced Carmelite tradition (Teresa and John) show the sacramental link between the mysticism of action, wisdom, and devotion.

The originality of this book lies in a close examination of John's life and writings using Raimundo Panikkar's tripartite model of salvation, namely the mystical paths of action (*karma yoga*), wisdom (*jñâna yoga*), and devotion (*bhakti yoga*). Panikkar borrows the terminology from the Hindu tradition. Yet, he sees the important roles that action, wisdom, and devotion play in the Christian mystical tradition by associating the path of action with apostolic service, the path of loving wisdom with sapiential mysticism, and the path of devotion and love with affective mysticism.

---

[8] F.C. Happold, *Mysticism: A Study and An Anthology* (New York: Penguin Books, 1988), 355.

Although Panikkar is a Catholic philosopher and theologian, he has regained for the West a holistic model using his knowledge of the Hindu tradition (especially the Advaita Vedanta and the *Bhagavad Gita*). In studying the Carmelite saint, it will be extremely helpful to consider Panikkar's theoretical framework as the focal point of this book by virtue of his tripartite model of salvation.

Panikkar saw the necessity to recover the tripartite human division of body (*soma*), soul (*psyche*), and spirit (*pneuma*) found in the Greco-Roman and in the Judeo-Christian traditions. Both traditions develop a philosophy of the person based on the belief that each human faculty forms an integral part of the whole, undivided self. For Christians, the notion that human beings are created in the image and likeness of God leads them to believe that they must take part in building the heavenly kingdom on earth.

Panikkar says that "each of us is an integral part of the higher and more real unity, the *Christus totus*."[9] Panikkar bases his theology on the trinitarian notion of *perichoresis* by referring to God, the world, and the human soul as sharing in oneness with one another. Panikkar explains his sacramental view of the universe, following St. Paul's and Teilhard's thoughts on the recapitulation of all things in Christ.

Panikkar's threefold anthropological division develops a typology that is best represented in the Hindu tradition by way of correlations, interrelations and interdependencies between the mystical paths of action, wisdom, and devotion. Each one of them corresponds to the different human faculties of body, soul, and spirit. At this point, it would be important to introduce Robert Neville's categories of the path of the soldier, sage, and saint as examples of how Protestant, Catholic, and Hindu thinkers share

---

[9] Raimundo Panikkar, *The Cosmotheandric Experience: Emerging Religious Consciousness* (Maryknoll, New York: Orbis Books, 1993), 56.

similarities in the way they interpret their rich philosophical and theological symbolic concepts.[10]

I am not taking these tripartite divisions in isolation from each other but rather I see them forming a unity-identity-whole. We find in Panikkar's typology the interaction between the mystical paths of body, soul, and spirit; *karma, jñâna* and *bhakti*; action, wisdom and devotion; earth, water and fire. Mystical union cannot be fully apprehended or comprehended without taking into consideration these three integral parts of the human condition. Panikkar claims that

> *[a]t this point, the word "contemplation" is appropriate. It has very little to do with such words as "deliberation," "reflection," or "theory." Contemplation is not a synthesis of action and theôria, of practice and theory, but it is the very ground where both practice and theory originate. Contemplation has both an intellectual and a practical aspect; thinking leads to a certain clarity, practice to a certain change of affairs. Contemplation is not a mixture of both; nor is it a synthesis; but it is this basic attitude where both knowledge and action have not yet been separated ... This is certainly the true, human experience. Contemplative life is neither pure meditation nor pure action; instead, it is the action upon which one reflects and the meditation upon which one acts, the undivided life. Its name is wisdom.*[11]

In the *Bhagavad-Gita*, Krishna instructs Arjuna on the eve of a battle how to control the egotistical desires without retiring from the worldly life. Arjuna is troubled by doubts concerning his duty as a warrior. Krishna suggests to Arjuna that total renunciation or withdrawal from worldly affairs is not a congruent path to salvation. Rather, Arjuna needs to learn how to act responsibly while he lives in the midst of a cosmic battle between good and evil, symbolically represented in the epic of the *Mahabharata* by the Pandava and the Kurava families.

---

[10] See Robert Neville, *Soldier, Sage, Saint* (New York: Fordham University Press, 1978).

[11] Raimon Panikkar, *A Dwelling Place for Wisdom* (Louisville, Kentucky: Westminster/John Knox Press, 1993), 62.

Nevertheless, the significance of going to war against the other family should be understood as a myth or as an allegory. In this way, the spiritual seeker finds meaning in the narrative by gaining new insights and wisdom about life. Then one realizes that the cosmic battlefield is a symbol that best represents Arjuna's spiritual battle with himself.

Arjuna is free to choose the course of action that will lead to slavery or to true liberation from all egotistical desires; however, to remain passive is still a choice. Thus, human beings cannot avoid being participants in the whole process of reaching salvation. Nonetheless, taking any course of action can be difficult if the seeker does not include right understanding, right attitude, or right knowledge in his or her spiritual journey. This could explain why the Brahmin caste system gives so much importance to the role of the priest in performing rituals as a sacred duty in life.

The *Gita* developed a code of morality by synthesizing all the important religious and philosophical teachings and values of India. The *Gita* came at a crucial historical moment in India during which Hindu, Buddhist, and Jain disciples were practicing extreme ascetic exercises, leading them apparently to withdrawing completely from the worldly life. Similarly, in St. John of the Cross's time extreme asceticism was the norm in religious circles. And yet, the same dangers appeared to be seen in both Catholic and Brahmanic societies when religious practitioners decided to completely withdraw from worldly activities. As a result of their passivity in confronting real life situations, tyrannical forces took control of religion and society in general.

The *Gita* contains a real ethical-social message directed to those spiritual seekers who, like Arjuna, live in a confused state, because they see contemplation and action as mutually exclusive. Broadly speaking, the *Gita*'s significance consists in renouncing the fruit of one's acts (known in Sanskrit as *phalatrsnavairagya*) without totally withdrawing from the world.

Comparatively, St. John of the Cross, in his mystical teachings, recommends following the path of spiritual detachment, of *la nada*, which is the path of self-negation in Christ. However, John's path of detachment does not end in self-negation, but instead the blessed soul enters the path of self-affirmation in Christ, or what John calls in his mystical theology, *el todo*. The *Gita* stresses purity of intention as something of the highest of nature's qualities while St. John of the Cross, being a Christian, had a similar goal in mind by preparing the soul to become pure in spirit.

The *Gita* is not an epic book about battlefields and wars intended to record well demonstrated historical facts. Otherwise, the *Gita* would have never been revered as a sacred scripture in India or elsewhere. The main appeal of the *Gita* lies precisely in its universality and timelessness. The twentieth century Indian sage, Mahatma Gandhi, understood the central message of the *Gita* as an allegory of the human journey into God. Like Gandhi, St. John of the Cross often warned the seeker to be cautious when he or she read his poems or used passages from the Bible "since the abundant meanings of the Holy Spirit cannot be caught in words."[12]

John recognized the ineffable character of the divine life, which cannot simply be put into words. He left his teachings open to multiple interpretations. Perhaps it is better understood now why the *Spiritual Canticle* was not included in the first collected edition. Some ecclesiastical authorities perceived John as a direct threat to the Catholic faith, in light of his new interpretations of biblical passages. Consider the great dangers that John might have posed to them, especially if we place his writings in the context of a Post-Tridentine Church which fiercely combatted and persecuted Lutherans and other heretical movements throughout all Europe.

Like the Bible, the *Gita* is a book full of stories. It is addressed to those human beings that need some guidance or instruction on how to become a true *yogin* in this life. That is to say, the teachings of the *Gita* present the seekers with the possibility of choosing from a variety of different paths that could lead them to salvation.

---

[12] John of the Cross, *The Collected Works of Saint John of the Cross*, trans. Kieran Kavanaugh and Otilio Rodríguez (Washington, District of Columbia: ICS Publications, 1991), 470; see *Spiritual Canticle,* Prologue, 1.

Additionally, mystics like John teach how to reach union with the divine in this life. The Carmelite saint understood that the ultimate goal of Christian mysticism is to reach union with the divine. The life of a friar or a nun prepares one to become more aware of this intimate union with God by practicing ascetic, moral, and spiritual disciplines such as fasting, nonviolence, and compassion toward all beings in the universe. In other words, the Christian way to salvation is attainable through right conduct (ethical dimension), right understanding (intellectual dimension), and right faith (spiritual dimension).

In the *Gita*, there are three major paths (*margas*) that religious seekers should master if they want to achieve union with the divine in this life. The spiritual paths are *karma mârga*, or the path of work, service and action which teaches the seeker how to be detached from the fruits of our good actions; *jñâna mârga*, or the path of intuitive knowledge which teaches the seeker how to acquire wisdom by becoming one with the divine; and *bhakti mârga*, or the path of love and devotion which teaches the seeker how to worship and please the divine.

In short, the *Gita* represents a unique synthesis of action, wisdom, and devotion. In other words, spiritual seekers ought to integrate these three paths of *yoga* in their lives.

One of the most important religious motifs in the comparative study of religions is the tripartite division of action, wisdom, and devotion, which can be found in all major world religious traditions. As Seyyed Hossein Nasr rightly observes:

> *There is also in religion a hierarchy of approaches to the Ultimate Reality which can again be summarized in a schematic fashion as the ways of work, love and knowledge, the already cited and famous karma marga, bhakti marga and jnana marga of Hinduism or al-makhafah, al-mahabbah, and al-ma'rifah of Islam. Likewise, there is a hierarchy among followers of religion or human types seen from the religious perspective corresponding to these modes of approach to the Ultimate Reality. It is to these types that the sapiential tradition of the ancient Greeks referred*

as the hylikoi, psychoi and pneumatikoi. Islam also distinguishes between the muslim, the mu'min as well as the possessor of spiritual virtue or ihsan, who is referred to in the Qur'an as muhsin, although this latter term is not as common in later religious literature as the first two.[13]

Raimundo Panikkar has recovered, for our Western religious consciousness, this threefold path to salvation (karma, jñâna, and bhakti), which he particularly inherited from the Hindu mystical tradition. Panikkar not only was influenced by the Hindu philosophico-mystical tradition as an intellectual enterprise, but he also incarnated in his flesh and bones the Hindu-Catholic cultures and faiths through his Hindu born father who was married to a Spanish Catholic woman. Moreover, Panikkar's typological model will help us better understand the thoughts of St. John of the Cross starting with chapter three.

Panikkar's notion of theandrism captures the religious imagination of the present writer because he offers a philosophical framework that perfectly fits into my study of St. John of the Cross. Panikkar defines theandrism as

> *una espiritualidad que combine en una síntesis auténtica las tres dimensiones de nuestra vida tanto en la tierra como en el cielo. En ella hay contemplación, que es algo más que pensamiento; acción, que no limita su horizonte a la construcción de la ciudad terrena, Dios, que no es únicamente un Juez o un Ojo escrutador; amor que sobrepasa todo sentimentalismo; oración, que no se limita a la petición ni siquiera a la alabanza sino que es también silencio, que no cae en la indiferencia; apofatismo, que no se estanca en nihilismo; gracia, que no es antinatural.*[14]

---

[13] S.H. Nasr, *The Need for a Sacred Science* (Albany, New York: State University of New York Press, 1993), 58-59.

[14] Raimon Panikkar, *La Trinidad y la Experiencia Religiosa* (Barcelona: Ediciones Obelisco, 1989), 117. The English translation of Panikkar's book is *The Trinity and the Religious Experience*. He writes:

In sum, Panikkar recapitulates his thoughts on the Hindu tripartite model for salvation by asserting the following:

Imagino que es por esto que la sabiduría de prácticamente todos los pueblos nos enseña que la apertura hacia la experiencia de Dios puede surgir:
- *a través del conocimiento (jñâna): por el esfuerzo de la inteligencia en trascenderse a sí misma;*
- *por el amor (bhakti): por el anhelo del corazón en buscar algo que le llene;*
- *a través de las obras (karma): por la creatividad de la creatura que quiere imitar al creador creando, esto es, haciendo.*[15]

It is time to study St. John of the Cross as a whole person, bringing together his multifaceted dimensions. Attention should be devoted to his active role in the Carmelite tradition as a religious reformer, an administrator, and a prophet; to his intellectual capacity as a mystical theologian and teacher; and to his religious devotion as a poet, friar, hermit, spiritual director, confessor, and priest.

Thus, by placing the SanJuanist mystical theology in its historical context and by reading his teachings as a whole (including life events, poems, and

---

A spirituality that combines in an authentic synthesis the three dimensions of our life [action, knowledge, and love] on earth as it is in heaven. In this spirituality we find contemplation that is something more than mere thought; action that it does not limit its horizon to building the earthly city; God that is not just a Judge or a scrutinizing Eye; love that is beyond all sentimentalism; prayer that is neither limited to petition nor to praise but is also silence that does not fall prey to indifference; apophatism that does not become nihilism; grace that is not antinatural. [my own translation]

[15] Raimon Panikkar, *La Experiencia de Dios* (Madrid: PPC, 1994), 93. In *The Experience of God* Panikkar writes,

I imagine that this is why the wisdom of practically all nations teaches us that the openness toward the experience of God can spring:
- *through knowledge (jñâna): by the effort of the intelligence in transcending itself;*
- *through love (bhakti): by the longing of the heart that is seeking something to feel alive;*
- *through works (karma): by the creature's creativity that desires to imitate the creator by creating, that is, by making.* [my own translation]

prose commentaries), one can gain a better understanding of John's life and writings. Otherwise, the SanJuanist text becomes a dogma, finding here and there fragments that could fit into our philosophical or theological system. Or as F.C. Happold succinctly puts it,

> To understand the doctrine of St. John of the Cross and to appreciate his breadth, one must read more than the famous chapter on detachment in The Ascent of Mount Carmel, and the descriptions of the two 'nights' in this book and in The Dark Night of the Soul; one must read also The Spiritual Canticle and The Living Flame of Love and the lovely lyrics of the spiritual quest, which take rank among the greatest mystical poems of all ages. If one does so, one will realize how well he deserves the description given of him by the twentieth-century Spanish poet, Antonio Machado: John of the Cross, spirit of ardent flame.[16]

Scholars in the field of mysticism are elaborating theories and methods for gaining better knowledge of the SanJuanist texts. As Janet Ruffing states:

> For academics to generate successful theories about mysticism, they must take into account a sufficient number of instances of the mystical element expressed sometimes in poetry, at other times in narratives, and at other times in treatises, along with descriptions and analyses of likely mistakes and dangers along the way. Considerations of genres, biographies, original audiences, the cultural and historical circumstances embedded in the texts (including power structures)--all require attention in developing adequate theories that can provide "explanations" that chasten and guide and correct the process of our understanding.[17]

The strict austere and abstruse picture of St. John of the Cross does not correspond to his legacy, for John's ascetico-mysticism is well-grounded in the best spirit of the Catholic tradition. As Peter Feldmeier says,

---

[16] Happold, *Mysticism*, 355-356.

[17] Janet Ruffing, "Introduction," in *Mysticism & Social Transformation*, 14.

> *A superficial reading of his works, especially in terms of his more dramatic teachings on detachment and leaving the world, gives many readers the impression that he was dualistic, or that he regarded all forms of sensory joy suspiciously. Arguably, there is language that seems to support this. Therefore, interpretation of his writings requires an attention to the facts of his life. He was surely an austere man, ascetical in many ways, and he was rigorous in his approach to the spiritual life. But he was also a gentle man, a man who loved the world generously and enjoyed it liberally.*[18]

Needless to say, SanJuanist scholars are in need of reinterpreting John's texts and his mystical thoughts in reference to the historical context in which he lived. Bringing out the multifaceted dimensions of St. John of the Cross illustrates more accurately the Carmelite saint's enormous contribution to the world. This study offers a new vision of St. John of the Cross as a contemplative mystic engaged in the socio-religious issues of his time.

The book presents a brief history of contemplation and action in the Christian mystical tradition and reviews the biography and writings of this Carmelite saint. Furthermore, it examines John's writings through appeal to Raimundo Panikkar's tripartite model of action, wisdom, and devotion. Finally, it concludes with an assessment of the SanJuanist legacy for today's world.

The first chapter provides a brief history of contemplation and prophetic action in the Christian mystical tradition. This chapter demonstrates that John's contemplative life is not divorced from the active life. John needs to be historically placed in the Christian mystical tradition where Martha and Mary are sisters. They complement each other. They both symbolize the mixed life by combining action and contemplation respectively. This study establishes the theoretical framework in an effort to better understand John as a contemplative in action.

---

[18] Peter Feldmeier, *Christianity Looks East: Comparing the Spiritualities of John of the Cross and Buddhaghosa* (New York: Paulist Press, 2006) 15.

Furthermore, it is important to examine the kind of mystic John was, and to establish the criteria formulated by the Christian mystical tradition (that of purgation, illumination, and union with God). Also, it is critical to compare and analyze John's mysticism with William James's philosophical criteria in his treatment of the validity of mystical experiences (namely, ineffability, noetic quality, transiency, and passivity).

The second chapter portrays St. John of the Cross in light of his dynamic, multifaceted life as a religious reformer, administrator, and writer, among many other roles. It places John in the historical context in which he lived to make clearer the reasons for his apparent silence about his personal involvement in the social and the religious issues of his time. In short, the importance of this chapter, although biographical in nature, is that it demonstrates the significance of John's life events in reference to his times and writings.

The third chapter introduces John's mystical path of action following Panikkar's holistic model. This chapter first examines John's thoughts on the active life and then studies John's views on the mixed life as the best possible way of integrating contemplation and action, solitude and solidarity, love of God and love of neighbor.

The fourth chapter explores John's intellectual and spiritual development within the Christian mystical tradition. His life before entering the Carmelite Order prepared him to live as a monk in the world. John demonstrated that the apparent dichotomy between the mystic and monk (so-called sacred) and the poet and writer (so-called secular) was no longer an issue for him, because he reconciled the sacred and the secular dimensions in himself.

For instance, John's use of sources proves how the Carmelite saint adopted in his mystical poetry the language of both secular (Góngora) and sacred (Song of Songs) texts. Additionally, this chapter traces some of the most influential schools of thought in John's writings and how these influences shaped his mystical language. Also, the medieval categories of *ratio* and *intellectus* are distinguished so that we can better understand the role of the intellect in John's mystical theology. And finally, this chapter explores the most misinterpreted and misplaced symbol in SanJuanist studies, namely John's mystical theology of the dark night.

The fifth chapter accounts for John's affective and devotional mysticism. For John, the goal of the Christian mystic is to become one with God. After achieving the state of *unio mystica*, the Christian is called to share the fruits of his contemplation with others. This chapter outlines John's mystical theology of love by revealing his views on the spiritual path of the heart.

The sixth chapter concludes with a few remarks about the vital messages that St. John of the Cross brings to the contemporary world. This chapter explores what the Carmelite saint has to offer to twenty-first century readers, and also comments on the philosophical and theological implications of seeing John as a contemplative in action.

1

CONTEMPLATION AND ACTION IN THE CHRISTIAN MYSTICAL TRADITION

To place St. John of the Cross within the Christian mystical tradition, one must understand the terms "mystical vision" and "prophetic voice." Christian mystics define mystical vision as the highest state of contemplation in this life. The mystic is one who has a direct experience of the divine. John defines mystical vision as the last step on the mystical ladder of divine love:

> *The tenth and last step of this secret ladder of love assimilates the soul to God completely because of the clear vision of God that a person possesses at once on reaching it ... [And] this vision is the cause of the soul's complete likeness to God. St. John says: We know that we shall be like him [1 Jn. 3:2], not because the soul will have as much capacity as God--this is impossible--but because all it is will become like God. Thus it will be called, and shall be, God through participation.*[1]

John concludes that the mystic who attains a vision of God in this life becomes like God by participation. As St. Paul states in the Bible, God shall be "all in all" (1 Cor. 15:28). Ultimately, the mystics become the embodiment of an authentic contemplative when they speak in God's name out of a living experience with the divine life.

---

[1] John of the Cross, *The Collected Works*, 445; *Dark Night* 2.20.5.

As a mystical theologian, John describes that contemplative or mystical state as an ascent to God. He writes: "Thus, by means of this mystical theology and secret love, the soul departs from itself and all things and ascends to God. For love is like a fire that always rises upward as though longing to be engulfed in its center."[2]

By prophetic voice the Christian mystics mean that prophets not only are entrusted with God's Word, but they also announce the deepest troubles of society by denouncing those who commit injustices against the suffering people, even at the expense of dying as martyrs themselves. In fact, many prophetic mystics were killed because they were serving God, even when they knew that their lives were in danger. In this regard, John says:

> *God truly grants the soul what it formally desired and what he promised it because the formal desire of the soul was not a manner of death but the service of God through martyrdom and the exercise of a martyr's love for him. Death through martyrdom in itself is of no value without this love, and God bestows martyrdom's love and reward perfectly by other means. Even though the soul does not die a martyr, it is profoundly satisfied since God has fulfilled its desire.*[3]

For John, the prophetic mystics are those who act in the world for the service and love of God. They are often called the friends or messengers of God. John understands that there is no greater love of God than the love of neighbor and the love of creation. Charity is the key element for those who are seeking eternal life. Without love, the seeker is condemned to live in darkness. Through love (*caritas*), the prophetic voice is linked to the path of apostolic action by serving God in all that he or she does, says, or thinks. As Susan Muto states:

St. John is not only recommending that we live a life of prayer; he also seems to be saying something bolder, namely, that we are to become living prayer. Eating, drinking, speaking or listening, resting or executing a task,

---

[2] Ibid; *Dark Night* 2.20.6.

[3] Ibid., 219; *Ascent* 2.19.13.

we can pray provided we "do so with desire for God and with [our] heart fixed on him." Thus do we loosen our fearful grasp on this short and passing life and come to enjoy true liberation. For us there is then no break between contemplation and action; one flows from and into the other.[4]

I will define "prophetic mysticism" in the historical context of the Judeo-Christian tradition, and especially following the lines established by John's Carmelite eremitical-prophetic tradition. Then, I will explain John's mediation between the contemplative and worldly active life following his mystical theology of final integration. I will select passages from John's writings to elucidate his theological commentaries on mysticism and prophecy.

Generally speaking, scholars and pietistic people tend to classify St. John of the Cross and other religious thinkers under the category of "contemplatives," "poets," or "inspiring authors." However, these categorizations into one group often overlook their active involvement in the world. As Janet Ruffing notes,

> One of the most important--though often neglected--theoretical issues related to types, descriptions, or definitions of mysticism and the mystical is the relationship of mysticism to prophecy or the prophetic. The connection between these two phenomena is rarely explicitly discussed, although it may be evoked in some communities, in some authors, and in some situations.[5]

The purpose of this book is precisely to shed light on the essential role that St. John of the Cross played in the history of Christianity by acknowledging both the mystical and the prophetic dimensions of his life testimonies and writings. The notion of prophetic mysticism is not altogether foreign to the Carmelite tradition, especially following the prophetic example of Elijah. This study will then explore the intrinsic relationship between the

---

[4] Susan Muto, *Words of Wisdom for our World: The Precautions and Counsels of St. John of the Cross* (Washington, D.C.: ICS Publications, 1996) 75.

[5] Janet Ruffing, "Introduction," in *Mysticism & Social Transformation*, 7.

prophetic and the mystical elements in the work of John of the Cross.

In the words of a great American religious philosopher, William E. Hocking:

> *The prophet must know himself; and he must know his world, not in detail but in so far as it is relevant to his purpose: such knowledge as this must come to him through his relation to the absolute. The prophet is but the mystic in control of the forces of history, declaring their necessary outcome: the mystic in action is the prophet. In the prophet, the cognitive certainty of the mystic becomes historic and particular; and this is the necessary destiny of that certainty: mystic experience must complete itself in the prophetic consciousness.*[6]

By "prophetic mysticism" I do not simply mean to foresee the future as it is frequently understood in popular circles. Rather, the prophetic mystic is one who bears witness to truth, justice, and love. In addition, the mystic in action develops what Hocking called "the prophetic consciousness." He asserts:

> *By the prophetic consciousness I do not mean a knowledge that something is to happen in the future, accomplished by forces beyond myself: I mean a knowledge that this act of mine which I now utter is to succeed and hold its place in history. It is an assurance of the future and of all time as determined by my own individual will, embodied in my present action. It is a power which knows itself to be such, and justly measures its own scope.*[7]

According to Wayne Teasdale, the prophetic voice demands witness and response to the most pressing moral and religious issues of our time:

> *The prophetic voice vigorously acknowledges the unjust events and policies that cause enormous tension, misery, and dislocation in the lives of countless numbers of people. War; the plight of refugees (most of whom*

---

[6] William E. Hocking, *The Meaning of God in Human Experience: A Philosophic Study of Religion* (New Haven, Connecticut: Yale University Press, 1955), 511.

[7] Ibid., 503.

> *are women and children); unjust economic, social, and political conditions that enrich a small class of rulers while oppressing the masses; threats to the environment--all are matters that should evoke the moral voice and our willingness to respond. We no longer have the luxury of ignoring the many challenges to justice in all its forms. We have a universal responsibility to apply the moral or prophetic function wherever we see justice disregarded, threats to world peace, oppression by states against its people or a neighboring nation, or some other danger as yet unforeseen.*[8]

Christians, like Jews, share a rich prophetic and mystical tradition throughout time. These two religious traditions are familiar with the many prophetic figures in ancient Israel who gave testimony to their special covenant with the Godhead (Abraham, Moses, Isaiah, Jeremiah, Elijah, Ezekiel, Hosea, Daniel, and many others). Incidentally, John's Carmelite Order adopted the Hebrew prophet Elijah as their spiritual founder and patron, although there was no direct historical link between them. The Carmelites saw Elijah as their spiritual role model because he balances the eremitical life and the prophetic life.

According to Peter Slattery,

> *The spirit, the personality, and the work of Elijah dominate the sacred site of Mount Carmel. In his prayer and reflection, the great prophet heard the call of God to bring his people back to him. With ardent zeal, prophetic courage, and a certain amount of passion he answered the call of God. The prophet is so present to God that God dominates his whole life. He is moved by the needs of the people who are being neglected and being misled ... In this way Carmelite spirituality encourages people to lie continually in the presence of God, and like the prophet, to be attentive to the signs of the times, so that they may hear the cry of the poor.*[9]

---

[8] Wayne Teasdale, *The Mystic Heart: Discovering a Universal Spirituality in the World's Religions* (Novato, California: New World Library, 1999), 157-158.

[9] Slattery, *The Springs of Carmel*, 136-137.

Besides Elijah, Moses best represents the archetype of the prophetic mystic in Judaism and Christianity. Although Moses never saw God face to face because God is not an object among other objects, he became a mystic by virtue of his personal encounter with God. Moses came down from Mt. Sinai to free his people from their enslaved state. Moses, the mystic visionary, became the prophetic exemplar for having received the direct revelations from Yahweh and for passing down the ten commandments to the Israelites. Yet it was Moses the prophet who raised his voice against the tyranny of Egypt against his people. He offered them a way out of their captivity by forcing them into a forty-year exodus in the desert.

What kind of mystical vision did Moses experience at Mount Sinai? Moses is a clear example of a mystic or visionary, though he never claimed to have seen God "face to face." He only saw his back, a symbol that could be interpreted as a metaphor of the hidden nature of the Godhead.

Mystics often adopt paradoxical symbols to describe the indescribable. The divine is so utterly mysterious that even those who are called the friends of God prefer to speak of "Him" in terms of divine attributes (cataphatic mystics) or they try to explain what God is not (apophatic mystics). Both Jewish and Christian mystics refuse to define God even when they had felt the presence of God within. By virtue of their conviction that God remains a mystery even in the aftermath of a mystic's experience, the prophetic mystic avoids idolatry by refusing to make God an idol.

The Godhead of the mystics is beyond any thought or word. Yet mystics are full of words to describe their personal experiences of the divine. The mystics cannot fully express in words and in thoughts the true nature of the Godhead; nonetheless, they are the ones who have gained immediate loving knowledge of God and have described for us the divine attributes or earthly manifestations of God. How would we know if God is merciful, compassionate, omnipresent, omniscient, eternal, just, and so forth, without someone experiencing those divine attributes?

Mystical theologians have clearly distinguished two kinds of vision: ordinary and mystical. When human beings look at the world using their senses, all creatures in the universe are seen as empirical realities or as identifiable objects. This kind of vision is called ordinary. However, mystical vision transcends the categories of time and space as most people often understand them. Reports from mystics show that those who have claimed to receive divine revelations did not identify the deity as a mere object.

Christians borrow from the Jewish tradition the archetypical image of Moses as the prophetic mystic par excellence. As a result, Christians follow the example of Moses in his prophetic response to the divine calling by sharing the fruits of his contemplation with the rest of the world. Thus, Christians believe vision must follow action. Otherwise the divine message never gets to the community and the mystic's response to God's plan is simply nullified by an act of cowardice, total passivity or rebellion. Therefore, action must be rooted in wisdom and divine knowledge, not vice versa. In short, the Judeo-Christian God demands from each believer cooperation in an effort towards building the heavenly kingdom on earth.

In the Christian mystical tradition, in which St. John of the Cross is deeply immersed, the contemplative and the prophetic are represented in the paradigmatic model of Mary-Martha. They are two aspects of the same reality. Mary of Bethany often symbolizes the contemplative mystic, while Martha best represents the active mystic. Mary and Martha are both sisters. They are seeing today as the Christian prototype of contemplatives in action.

The biblical sources play an essential role in understanding the Christian message of St. John of the Cross because his contemplative desire to become one with God ultimately led him to embrace the world in his apostolic ministry. The biblical passage that creates the apparent dichotomy between contemplation and action in Christian circles comes from the Gospel of Luke. Jesus, answering to Martha's inquiry about why her sister Mary has left her to serve alone, says: "Martha, Martha, you are anxious and troubled about many things; but one thing is needed, and Mary has chosen that good part, which shall not be taken away from her" (Luke 10:41-42).

Some Christians have interpreted that passage as if Mary, who symbolically represents the life of contemplation, chose the best life. Such biblical interpreters believe the passage devalues the life of action, which is depicted in the story of Martha. But Jesus never rejected the life of action. On the contrary, Jesus lived a very active life in his own time.

Perhaps the biblical passage from Luke could historically be interpreted as an attempt to break with some of the patriarchal norms in the established Jewish society that for so long had put women down by subordinating them to the offices of housekeeper, wife, and mother. Instead, the religion of Jesus allowed women to study and discuss the social and religious issues of their time with men. Women acquired important roles within the Jesus movement. And that influence lasted for a few centuries until the Christian religion adopted the patriarchal, hierarchical model of the Roman Empire.

The exegetical problem that Luke's biblical passage poses to the Christian tradition is whether or not Jesus intended to reject the active life altogether. Maybe Jesus clearly saw the unfair treatment towards women and tried to raise awareness by letting women sit among his disciples and followers. It could be inferred from a careful reading of the Gospel of Luke that Jesus encouraged women to participate in the meetings if they wished. Otherwise, why did Jesus allow Mary to sit at his feet and hear his word when her duty as a Jewish woman was to take care of the household? (Luke 10:39). Clearly, Jesus allowed women to participate and discuss important issues within his movement, even to the point of letting them take leadership roles in his sect. In addition, women played a crucial role as witnesses of Jesus' passion, death, and resurrection.

The other historical problem that Christians faced in the past, and one that still is a debatable question in some Catholic and Protestant circles, is whether or not active apostolic work by and of itself is conducive to a more perfect union with God, and thereby leads practitioners to salvation. In the history of Christianity there are those who see action as a way to salvation, notably the martyrs. These and other Christians seek the road to salvation by taking the path of action.

However, the paradigmatic models of contemplatives in action today are Jesus of Nazareth, Bartolomé de las Casas, Saint Ignatius of Loyola, Saint Teresa of Ávila, Teilhard de Chardin, Dorothy Day, Martin Luther King, Jr., Dietrich Bonhoeffer, Thomas Merton, and Oscar Romero, among others. These Christians found God in all things. They thought of apostolic service, which resulted from mystical graces from God, as a peculiar way of prayer and as a way of worshipping the Lord.

Each one of them stood up as prophetic witnesses to justice and peace in their unique ways, asking for forgiveness and reconciliation in a time when they were fighting against all odds inside and outside the Church. They all responded out of their love of God and their love of neighbor so that they could heal the wounds of those who suffered persecution, torture, and death, the *anawim*.

Without doubt, the prophetic mystics did not turn their backs to the suffering inflicted on millions of people in different parts of the world. They did not withdraw completely from society in search for solitude alone. Instead, they protested against the individual and structural evils of their respective societies. Their spirituality was based on the ideal of building a compassionate world, including the love of the enemy. In the words of Wayne Teasdale:

Socially engaged spirituality is the inner life awakened to responsibility and love. It expresses itself in endless acts of compassion that seek to heal others, contributing to the transformation of the world and the building of a nonviolent, peace-loving culture that includes everyone.[10]

Although apostolic action raised to the level of the service for God was a spiritual practice, Christian mystics recognized that action alone did not lead them to salvation. Action can be blind if the vision of the faithful is

---

[10] Teasdale, *The Mystic Heart*, 239.

not rooted in God's plan for humanity. In fact, there is the danger of relying too much on blind (or even experiential) faith when the blessed soul thinks he or she has arrived. By "arriving" I mean that the mystic might think he or she is no longer responsible for his or her future actions because they have been touched by God's love, which redeem all blessed souls from their sinful state. This way of thinking could lead to quietistic and passive behaviors which are not conducive to an apostolic ministry based on the love of neighbor and the love of God.

Liberation theologians like Segundo Galilea or Gustavo Gutiérrez have contributed a great deal in our time to recovering the prophetic element of Christianity. They have studied the life of the mystics and identified their prophetic dimension. For instance, Segundo Galilea was really interested in the study of the Spanish mystics, especially of St. Ignatius of Loyola, St. Teresa of Ávila, and St. John of the Cross. Galilea saw the Spanish mystics as great contemplatives in action, or as prophetic mystics. He writes:

> *The service of the kingdom is the point at which the great mystics of the 16th century converge in their presentation of the ideal practice of effective love. All of them assumed responsibility in facing the history and needs of their time, and responded to them with a lucid and faithful Christian practice. In this respect they were prophets and their service of the kingdom was not ordinary, but prophetic. A prophet is a person who discerns the signs of the times in order to undertake the attitude and the response which the Spirit wills. Prophetism is an eminent form of the practice of effective charity.*[11]

Galilea was well aware of the religious and cultural context of sixteenth century Spain. He knew that the Spanish culture was closely linked to the church. Their form of government could be interpreted as a theocratic model because the modern separation of church and state did not exist at that time. King Phillip II was appointed as head of the Spanish church. He

---

[11] Segundo Galilea, *The Future of Our Past: The Spanish Mystics Speak to Contemporary Spirituality* (Notre Dame, Indiana: Ave Maria Press, 1985), 64-65.

expanded the domains of the kingdom of Castile and Aragon to the four corners of the world. No empire saw the mighty power of a kingdom as strong as the Spanish. He ruled the Spanish society for several decades. He spread God's Word by forcing mass conversion on the conquered people. At the same time, the Vatican exercised great influence on the domestic and international policies of the Spanish king. The Pope gave the monarch physical, moral and spiritual support, sending missionaries to the conquered lands.

Galilea also recognized the social and religious reform taken by the Spanish mystics. The mystics played such an important role because they sanctified not only themselves but also the world. The Spanish mystics were not too worried about their own personal salvation. Their religious commitment was a testimony to their social awareness in a time of great troubles, especially in their mission of establishing religious monastic centers and universities. Both Jesuits and Carmelites were well known for their religious centers of prayer and for their missionary foundations all over the world. Even in the sixteenth century, Spanish missionaries included travels to Europe, Africa, Asia and the Americas. Galilea points out that

> *Ignatius, Teresa and John of the Cross have the same attitude and the same prophetic practice: to join extreme fidelity and adherence to the church with a practice featuring not words or criticisms, but rather, daring and significant deeds aimed at reforming the church from within. Their prophetism also manifests itself in their distrust in resorting to temporal means and powers and in their insistence above all on evangelical conversion and on the personal and collective holiness of the church.*[12]

Gustavo Gutiérrez, the founding father of liberation theology, was also interested in the Spanish mystics. He saw them as prophetic figures responding with their loving wisdom to the signs of the time. Having in mind the Spanish mystics, he says:

---

[12] Ibid., 65.

> *A particular spirituality always represents a reorganizing of the fundamental foci of Christian life, on the basis of a central intuition or insight. The intuition is that of great men and women of the Spirit as they respond to the needs and demands of their age. Every spirituality is a way that is offered for the greater service of God and others: freedom to love.*[13]

The language of the Spanish Carmelites combines the mystical tradition of love with prophetic denunciation (as the ancient prophets did before them). According to Donald W. Buggert,

> *One can be prophet only because one first tastes the divine. Prophets experience the divine absence or dis-grace in history only because they first experience the divine presence or grace. This experience of the divine presence compels the prophet to denounce its absence, the reign of Satan, and to announce a new future, the reign of God. Because prophets first stand in the sight of the living God, they are filled with zeal for the Lord God of Hosts ... And so with this God, one can only be a contemplative prophet, not a contemplative or a prophet. We must beware of a "contemplative Docetism," an ahistorical contemplation. As Gustavo Gutiérrez cautions, we must not set a "praxis of heaven" against a "praxis of earth" and vice versa.*[14]

In other words, the mystic and the prophet are not two separate beings. Rather, the mystic in action integrates both the mystical and the prophetic elements in himself or herself. Hence it is that mystics like St. John of the Cross or St. Teresa of Ávila who have greatly contributed to their world by founding new monasteries and convents, reforming the Carmelite tradition, and inspiring those who follow them through their teachings and writings. Clearly, their actions are the working effects of God's love in

---

[13] Gustavo Gutiérrez, *We Drink from Our Own Wells: The Spiritual Journey of a People*, trans. Matthew J. O'Connell (Maryknoll, New York: Orbis Books, 1984), 89.

[14] Donald W. Buggert, "The Contemplative as Iconoclast," in *Carmel and Contemplation: Transforming Human Consciousness*, eds. Kevin Culligan and Regis Jordan (Washington, District of Columbia: ICS Publications, 2000), 62-63.

them. Similarly, Gustavo Gutiérrez describes the intrinsic relationship between the mystical and the prophetic elements in terms of language: "Mystical language expresses the gratuitousness of God's love, prophetic language expresses the demands this love makes."[15]

Thus, in the Judeo-Christian tradition, there is no clear gap between the mystical and the prophetic consciousness. The roles of the prophet and the mystic often intertwine. The mystic is the person who has a direct experience of God; the prophet is that person who, after having a vision of the divine, takes the initiative by partaking in the activities of the world without clinging to his or her own actions. The mystic has a vision of the divine; the prophet gives voice to that vision so that he or she becomes a witness and a vessel of truth, justice, and love in the world. The mystic is personally transformed by his or her encounter with the divine; the prophet attaches great importance to social commitment by becoming a "messenger" or "friend" of God. The mystic seeks out personal salvation; the prophet searches for the welfare of the community and the world at large. The mystic withdraws from the world to return more fully equipped to the world as a prophet, fully engaged and involved in his or her social environment. The mystic therefore is a spiritual master, a seeker of the really Real; the prophet fulfills the task of a social and/or religious reformer, who is committed to building the kingdom of God on earth by fully conforming to God's vision for the world.

The "healthy" mystic returns to the worldly activities fully equipped after having received special revelations from the divine. At this meeting point, the mystic becomes the prophet. And interestingly enough, the genuine prophet is first of all a mystic, a messenger of God. He or she will not stop working until the message is delivered and implemented. According to José-María Vigil, "the prophet listens to the living God and then speaks in

---

[15] Gustavo Gutiérrez, *On Job,* trans. Matthew J. O'Connell (Quezon City, Philippines: Claretian Publications, 1987), 95.

God's name."¹⁶

> *Vigil defines the prophet as*
> *- the person who speaks "in a name";*
> *- the person who consoles;*
> *- the person who challenges and proclaims;*
> *- the person who anticipates the people's march towards salvation, sustains it and speeds it up.*¹⁷

Genuine prophetic mystics (or mystical prophets) are those who commit themselves to an unrestricted desire to love God and persevere in their courageous effort to better serve the community and the world at large by sharing the fruits of their actions. As Livia Kohn puts it,

> *The accomplished mystic, finally, is the sage. Described as the Great Man [the New Man in the Christian tradition], he is ruler, shaman, and sage merged into one. He returns to life in the world and serves his fellow beings as teacher, guide, and ruler ... The accomplished mystic is thus a true human being, a perfected or realized one, who is whole within himself; easily communicates with the world above; and has a responsible role in the political and social order of his time.*¹⁸

By studying the life and thoughts of the prophetic mystics one might realize that the mystics' actions spring from a deep contemplative life in which apostolic service is seen as an extension of their prophetic life. Christian mystical theologians traditionally understood the story of Martha and Mary as two complementary aspects of the divine life, the active and the contemplative. As Thomas Merton rightly observes:

> *Contemplation and action necessarily have their part in every religious Rule. The two must always go together, because Christian perfection is*

---

[16] Pedro Casaldáliga and José María Vigil, *Political Holiness* (Maryknoll, New York: Orbis Books, 1994), 125.

[17] Ibid., 124.

[18] Livia Kohn, *Early Chinese Mysticism: Philosophy and Soteriology in the Taoist Tradition* (Princeton, New Jersey: Princeton University Press, 1992), 164-165.

> *nothing else but the perfection of charity, and that means perfect love of God and of men ... But the active Orders would soon find that their activity was sterile and useless if it were not nourished by an interior spirit of prayer and contemplation, while the contemplative who tries to shut out the needs and sufferings of humanity and isolate himself in a selfish paradise of interior consolations will soon end up in a desert of sterile illusion.*[19]

Merton did stress the importance of the contemplative life over the active life because the "supreme apostolate" of his own monastic order, the Cistercians, is "the contemplation of God" (35). Nonetheless, Merton was well aware of the need for the monk to reach out to those who suffer in this world. Prayer without charity, he says, is a "sterile illusion."

Similarly, the Carmelites claimed in the past the same type of reasoning. St. Teresa and St. John of the Cross brought with them a renewed sense of what the Carmelite Order stands for by returning to the primitive spirit of Carmel which includes both the contemplative (or eremitical) life and the active (or apostolic) life. Thus, the Carmelite desert experience of silence and solitude led their mystics to become more aware of their special relationship with other creatures and the whole creation.

Merton, following the lines developed by the Christian mystics (especially by Gregory the Great, St. Bernard of Clairvaux, and the Carmelite reformers), says of contemplation that it is "the highest expression of the monastic and Christian lives, but it rests on action and tends to overflow in apostolic activity for souls."[20]

Echoing the great Fathers of the Church, Merton saw a continuity of thought with the traditional teachings of the Church. He declared that apostolic action ought to go hand in hand with the life of interior prayer because charity ultimately is an extension of the contemplative life. Merton

---

[19] Thomas Merton, *The Waters of Siloe* (New York: Image Books, 1962), 31-32.

[20] Thomas Merton, *On Saint Bernard* (Kalamazoo, Michigan: Cistercian Publication, 1980), 34.

argues that "[a]ction and contemplation together are expressions of this life of the Church. They both flow from our life in Christ."[21]

Genuine mystics in action are those who are able to integrate a contemplative love for the glory and honor of God and an apostolic and social commitment for our neighbor and for all creation. As William Johnston declares in *The Inner Eye of Love*:

> *I believe that the great prophets were mystics in action-- their inner eye was awakened so that they saw not only the glory of God but also the suffering, the injustice, the inequality, the sin of the world. This drove them into action and often led to their death. And just as the great prophets were mystics, so the great mystics had a prophetic role.*[22]

St. John of the Cross followed the tradition of contemplatives in action like St. Ignatius of Loyola, although his role as a contemplative was tied to an apostolate of prayer. Conversely, St. Ignatius of Loyola was seen by many as a man of action or as a soldier of Christ since he was the founder of the Jesuit Company. Yet Ignatius has been gaining more recognition as a mystic and contemplative thanks to Karl Rahner's and Harvey Egan's studies.

John received his training as a contemplative in action from two main sources. First, of course, was the example set by his Carmelite tradition which strives to achieve a perfect balance between the eremitical (or contemplative) life and the missionary (or active) life. The second major influence was the legacy left by those who he had the fortune to meet or to follow throughout his life, especially St. Teresa of Ávila, St. Juan de Ávila, and St. Ignatius of Loyola, among other distinguished religious leaders.

St. John of the Cross, as the cofounder member of the Discalced Carmelite tradition initiated by St. Teresa of Ávila, best exemplified the spirit of the mixed life. They both brought together the life of contemplation, which

---

[21] Ibid., 27.

[22] William Johnston, *The Inner Eye of Love: Mysticism and Religion* (San Francisco: Harper & Row, Publishers, 1982), 11. William Johnston further says that "mysticism overflows into activity" (25).

has as its goal a more perfect union with God through the daily practice of prayer following the eremitical model of the Carmelite tradition, and the life of apostolic action, which translates John's and Teresa's mystical vision into the realm of worldly activities. Nevertheless, there are commentators who saw the Carmelite tradition merely as a contemplative religious order. As E.W. Trueman Dicken notes:

> *Despite the Western origin of the Crusaders, the spiritual and monastic atmosphere of the Kingdom of Jerusalem had been largely that of the Eastern Church, and the life of the early Carmelites drew much from the traditions of Scete and Nitria. They lived as solitaries, bound together by their common eucharist and by the strict obedience enjoined by their rule. In the Eastern Church the notion of 'active' Religious orders is virtually unknown, and the weighty emphasis upon contemplation in the primitive Carmelite community is thus no more than one might expect to find.*[23]

But did the Teresian reform follow the primitive Carmelite spirit in the lines interpreted by Trueman Dicken? Most certainly not. Merton clearly understood the role of prophetic mysticism in the Spanish Carmelites when he declared: "Unless I am much mistaken, it was St Teresa and the Carmelite mystics of the sixteenth century who first brought into prominence the apostolic role and fruitfulness of the pure contemplative."[24]

John wholly embraced a mystical theology of holiness in action by taking care of administrative businesses; serving as a spiritual director, priest, or

---

[23] E.W. Trueman Dicken, *The Crucible of Love: A Study of the Mysticism of St. Teresa of Jesus and St. John of the Cross* (New York: Sheed and Ward, 1963), 8.

[24] Merton, *On Saint Bernard*, 61. The Carmelite reform is a perfect example of how central it is for Teresa and John to live a balanced life between interior prayer and apostolic action. As Merton observes in his essay, *What to Do-The Teaching of St. John of the Cross*:

> *The words of St. John of the Cross must be understood in the context of the saint's own life. He was not preaching an absolute repudiation of all duties and responsibilities and all works and labours for the Church of God or for other men. He and St. Teresa of Avila, the greatest contemplatives of their time, were also very active and laboured and suffered much for the reform of the Carmelite Order* (What is Contemplation?, 68).

confessor; fulfilling his poetic talent and theological vocation. In other words, John consecrated his life to God by unfolding a special love for the world and for all creatures living in it.

Was John a mystic? What kind of mystic was he? How did John define mysticism and prophecy? John was certainly a mystic because he had a direct experience with the divine. John's poetry is impregnated with many mystical symbols from the living flame of love to the dark night. John's theological commentaries also bear witness to the mystical dimension of the Carmelite saint, especially in his attempt to explain the unexplainable. In other words, John was both an apophatic and a cataphatic mystic. He used poetry as a medium to express that which cannot be fully expressed. And yet, John was comfortable affirming the immanence of God in creation through gazing at the divine attributes (namely, omnipresence, omnipotence, omniscience, eternity, and many others).

John explicitly defined mysticism as contemplation when he said: "For contemplation is nothing else than a secret and loving inflow of God, which if not hampered, fires the soul in the spirit of love."[25] He also defined contemplation as "an inflow of God into the soul, which purges it of its habitual ignorances and imperfections, natural and spiritual, and which the contemplatives call infused contemplation or mystical theology."[26]

For John, the mystic is not simply someone who is seeking union with God but rather someone who has already experienced the loving wisdom of

---

[25]John of the Cross, *The Collected Works*, 382; *Dark Night* 1.10.6. St. John of the Cross's definition followed that of Pseudo-Dionysius when the latter defined contemplation in the *Mystical Theology* 1.1. as "a ray of darkness."

[26] Ibid., 401; *Dark Night* 2.5.1. For St. John of the Cross infused contemplation meant experiential faith, or union with God. The SanJuanist dark night of faith is the meeting point where "God supernaturally illumines the soul with the ray of his divine light" (*Ascent* 2.2.1). We know the Living God by unknowing. For John, therefore, faith was "that admirable means of advancing to God, our goal" (*Ascent* 2.2.1). "Faith, the theologian says, is a certain and obscure habit of soul" (*Ascent* 2.3.1). In short, faith is "a dark night for souls, but in this way it gives them light" (*Ascent* 2.3.4).

God at the deepest center of his or her soul. John lived his mystical experience of intimacy with God with great intensity. His devotional poems clearly illustrate his purpose of guiding the spiritual seeker to achieve union with God in this life.

This spiritual journey in search of union with God is better expressed in his celebrated poem, the *Ascent of Mount Carmel*. But it is in his poems, the *Spiritual Canticle* and the *Living Flame of Love*, where John fully expressed his deep intimate union with God using the nuptial imagery of the spiritual marriage between the lover and the beloved.

As a mystical theologian, John identified the highest degree of mystical union in this life with infused contemplation. Ultimately, it is only God who could grant the gift of grace to the human soul, although Christians prepare themselves to receive God within by fasting, meditating, or doing apostolic work for the service of God.

John claimed that the mystical vision of God "is proper to the intellect."[27] Following Aquinas's epistemology, John explained his theory of divine knowledge and union with God through the concept of active and passive intellect. For him, the intellect was not associated with the rational faculty of the human soul but rather with intuitive understanding, category which belongs to the realm of mystical theology.

Moreover, this experiential loving wisdom was defined by John as the highest state of contemplation in this life. The blessed soul was able to hear the still small voice of God. "These are pure spiritual revelations or visions which are given only to the spirit without the service and help of the senses,"[28] as John observes.

> St. John of the Cross was a Christian mystic because he adopted the mystical language of Christianity as his own experience. He writes: "Insofar as infused contemplation is loving wisdom of God, it produces

---

[27] Ibid., 531; *Spiritual Canticle* 14.14.

[28] Ibid; *Spiritual Canticle* 14.15.

> *two principal effects in the soul: by both purging and illumining, this contemplation prepares the soul for union with God through love.*[29]

Thus, the Carmelite saint, being rooted in the Christian mystical tradition, identified the purgative, illuminative, and unitive as the three stages of the mystical life.

The purgative stage corresponds to the beginners (or "*principiantes*"). John understood purgation as a spiritual discipline in which one prepares the soul to receive God by practicing asceticism. The ascetic person seeks God by fasting or praying. At the same time, the Christian monastic tradition requires from the practitioner or spiritual seeker great discipline and human effort (acquired contemplation). As a result of this effort, God will purge the human soul of all its bad habits (infused contemplation). John writes: "If you desire that devotion be born in your spirit and that the love of God and the desire for divine things increase, cleanse your soul of every desire, attachment, and ambition in such a way that you have no concern about anything."[30]

The illuminative stage corresponds to the proficient ones (or '*aprovechados*'). The religious believer desires to know God. And with God's help, the seeker will experience union with God in this life by virtue of his or her own degree of receptivity of the divine light within. He or she who has been blessed by God will have the opportunity to know the hidden mystery of God. According to John, "a revelation is nothing else than the disclosure of some hidden truth, or the manifestation of some secret or mystery, as when God imparts understanding of some truth to the intellect, or discloses to the soul something that he did, is doing, or is thinking of doing."[31]

God infuses wisdom and understanding to those who receive the divine life in their hearts. As John puts it, "God supernaturally illumines the soul

---

[29] Ibid.

[30] Ibid., 91; *Sayings of Light and Love*, 78.

[31] Ibid., 244; *Ascent* 2.25.1.

with the ray of his divine light. This light is the principle of the perfect union that follows after the third night."[32] In another passage, John states:

> *Jeremiah shows clearly that the soul is purged by the illumination of this fire of loving wisdom (for God never bestows mystical wisdom without love, since love itself infuses it) where he says: He sent fire into my bones and instructed me [Lam. 1:13]. And David says that God's wisdom is silver tried in the fire [Ps. 11:6], that is, in the purgative fire of love. This contemplation infuses both love and wisdom in each soul according to its capacity and necessity. It illumines the soul and purges of its ignorance, as the Wise Man declares it did to him* [Ecclesiasticus. 51:25-27].[33]

Finally, the unitive or transformative mystical stage belongs to the perfect or blessed souls (or '*perfectos*'). The goal of the Christian mystic is to become one with God. But this mystical union is only possible by grace, not by nature. The human soul becomes God by participation. The one who is reborn in the Holy Trinity will be able to see the kingdom of God, which is the highest state of perfection in this life. Yet God and the human soul remain separated, although united by the bonds of this mutual love. As John explains in his theological commentaries:

When God grants this supernatural favor to the soul, so great a union is caused that all the things of both God and the soul become one in participant transformation, and the soul appears to be God more than a soul. Indeed, it is God by participation. Yet truly, its being (even though transformed) is naturally as distinct from God's as it was before, just as the window, although illumined by the ray, has being distinct from the ray's.[34]

John's mystical language of union echoes the experience of the Desert Fathers and the Greek Orthodox Christians, especially in their theology of participation (or *theosis*). As John points out, "[h]aving been made one with

---

[32] Ibid., 156; *Ascent* 2.2.1.

[33] Ibid., 422; *Dark Night* 2.12.2.

[34] Ibid., 165; *Ascent* 2.5.7.

God, the soul is somehow God through participation. Although it is not God as perfectly as it will be in the next life, it is like the shadow of God."[35]

Let me clarify one important thing about this SanJuanist teaching in regard to how these three mystical stages or ways to God are intertwined at all levels in their *unio mystica*. Clearly John did not say that the purgative, the illuminative and the unitive must follow a linear understanding in the spiritual map traced by him and other mystical theologians before him. As a matter of fact, it is God through His/Her infused, loving grace and wisdom who ultimately purges the human soul from all imperfections, who illumines the soul by reflecting the divine rays of light within and around oneself, and who unites the human soul to God by becoming God by participation as co-partakers in building the kingdom of God here on earth.

All in all, the culmination of the mystical journey towards God is at last celebrated in John's poems with with his famous verses stressing the spiritual marriage between the lover and the beloved, often forgotten among the lilies in their total absorption of the human soul into the Godhead as if they two are merged at least in a brief but lasting moment of divine intimacy, friendship and erotic love that transcends all senses and yet sees the Divine presence dwelling in all things. Unfortunately for the mystic, this beautiful encounter with ultimate reality does not last forever, although God transforms the human soul *a lo divino* (in a divine manner), so this lasting memory at the deepest center of the human soul gives the mystic a taste of eternal life and brings joy, wisdom and hope in this life and the next life to come.

However, one could ask the following question: how does someone know that a mystic is truly experiencing God and not something else? In other words, how do philosophers distinguish a true mystical state from a pseudo-mystical state?

---

[35] Ibid., 706; *Living Flame of Love* 3.78.

William James answers this question in his philosophical treatment of the two types of religious experience: the once-born and the twice-born. The main distinction of the two types is "their different attitude toward evil and toward the place of volitional effort."[36] For James, morality is the factor that allows him to take account of the evil in the world.

James identifies four distinguishing marks common to all authentic mystics' reports: ineffability, noetic quality, transiency, and passivity. For James, the ineffable character of the mystical experience shares a universal, common thread in the history of mysticism. The mystic allegedly has a direct personal encounter with the divine that is in a paradoxical sense incommunicable. Any attempt to describe the mystical experience will fail since "no adequate report of its content can be given in words."[37]

However, the mystic often attempts to articulate his or her own mystical experiences in writing. There are vast amounts of literature on the subject. Most of the time the mystic does not fully know or understand the divine message. Nevertheless, the mystic becomes a sort of philosopher or theologian in search of explanations that might help him or her decodify the message.

Mystics also report that their mystical or altered states of consciousness provide them with some cognitive value. The mystic gains wisdom and knowledge by virtue of this human-divine encounter. The mystical experience has a noetic quality since it conveys "states of knowledge,"[38] resulting in a deeper insight and understanding into the nature of things. This kind of trans-rational knowledge is by no means irrational. This experiential knowledge has an authoritative validity for the person to whom the divine mysteries of the universe have been revealed. For James, these noetic qualities are manifested through revelations (or epiphanies),

---

[36] John M. Moore, *Theories of Religious Experience: With Special Reference to James, Otto and Bergson* (New York: Round Table Press, 1938), 48.

[37] William James, *The Varieties of Religious Experience* (New York: Penguin Books, 1985), 380.

[38] Ibid., 380.

illuminations, and mystical visions. Wisdom is acquired either in the form of dreams or in deep contemplative states of the soul.

Transient experiences are typically characteristic of the mystical state of consciousness. These states rarely last very long. At most, James says, they last two hours. However, the mystical experience extends over a whole life leaving a permanent mark in the human soul, especially in the memory. For James, a genuine mystical experience has a transformative quality allowing the seer to look at the world in new ways. The mystic is wholly transformed by this human-divine encounter. This spiritual transformation is what the Christian tradition calls *metanoia* (change of heart).

Finally, the mystic feels "grasped and held by a superior power."[39] These moments are always experienced as a gift, as something given. This passive state is what Christian mystical theologians called infused contemplation. However, this state of passivity does not lead to quietism. The mystic must act according to the divine plan. He or she feels the burden of being blessed. The blessed soul is called now to act in the world. Moral courage and spiritual integrity are essential qualities that the mystic must possess if he or she follows the divine commandment.

For James, the great contribution of the mystics lies not so much in their personal accounts of the divine, but rather in their moral conduct. James's pragmatism is tested by the simple Christian formula, "Therefore by their fruits you will know them" (Matthew 7:20). Furthermore, James saw St. Ignatius of Loyola as an exemplar of a contemplative in action, and St. John of the Cross as one of the best mystical teachers in the history of the Catholic Church.

Some commentators, however, have criticized James because either his marks are wide enough to fit many experiences that are far from being mystical (Harvey Egan), or his marks are too few to give a fuller account of the mystical state (Evelyn Underhill). Additionally, James was criticized by some commentators because he was a religious pluralistic thinker who

---

[39] Ibid., 381.

conceded validity to different truth-claims of the divine that had their origins in other places and times besides Christianity. For these critics, however, there can be only one reality that is holy. For Egan, of course, Christianity is the ultimate form of truth.

Let me now consider James's theory of the validity of religious experience. James rejected the "medical materialists" of his time because they (mostly psychologists) reduced mystical experiences to deviant behavior as a way of escapism. He says:

> *Medical materialism finishes up Saint Paul by calling his vision on the road to Damascus a discharging lesion of the occipital cortex, he being an epileptic. It snuffs out Saint Teresa as an hysteric, Saint Francis of Assisi as an hereditary degenerate. George Fox's discontent with the shams of his age, and his pining for spiritual veracity, it treats as a symptom of a disordered colon. Carlyle's organ-tones of misery it accounts for a gastro-duodenal catarrh.*[40]

James thought that "medical materialists" undermined the spiritual authority of those mystical figures mentioned in his passage. He further said that the explanations of "medical materialists" ought not to be taken seriously since they do not illuminate all cases. Nevertheless, there have been reports from mystics who suffered mental problems claiming that they were genuine mystics. Therefore, we are in need of criteria that will distinguish mystics from pseudo-mystics.

What are then, for James, the criteria of the validity of religious experience? James gave a concise answer to that question: "Immediate luminousness, in short, philosophical reasonableness, and moral helpfulness are the only available criteria."[41] In other words, James believed that the mystic who has received infused knowledge from the divine must first be aware of this mystical encounter. And this acknowledgment must be accompanied by making sure that the mystic understands the divine message and

---

[40] Ibid., 13.

[41] Ibid., 18.

takes full responsibility as a moral agent in the task of fulfilling God's plan.

In a different passage, James suggests that "[c]onsciousness of illumination is for us the essential mark of 'mystical' states."[42] Thereby, James's theory of pragmatism demonstrates the validity of his criterion by putting forward a verification system in action that constantly examines the mystics' accounts based upon their deeds and explanations.

In regard to what kind of authority comes out of James's theory of the validity of religious experience, there are three clear statements:

(1) Mystical states, when well developed, usually are, and have the right to be, absolutely authoritative over the individuals to whom they come.

(2) No authority emanates from them which should make it a duty for those who stand outside of them to accept their revelations uncritically.

(3) They break down the authority of the non-mystical or rationalistic consciousness, based upon the understanding and the senses alone. They show it to be only one kind of consciousness. They open out the possibility of other orders of truth, in which, so far as anything in us vitally responds to them, we may freely continue to have faith.[43]

James claimed that mystical states have no authority over other people simply because they are based only on scientific reports. He left us with other avenues of exploration that perhaps cannot scientifically be verified. Furthermore, James gave credit to the mystics' reports because they provide meaning and hope to those who believe in them. For James, "the mystic is, in short, invulnerable, and must be left, whether we relish it or not, in undisturbed enjoyment of his creed."[44] As a result, James rejected the scientific materialism of his age, which reduced everything to the study of the senses alone or to that which can be demonstrated by reason.

---

[42] Ibid., 408.

[43] Ibid., 423.

[44] Ibid., 424.

There is no question in James's mind that mystical experiences are usually true to those who have them. Nonetheless, the question is whether they have the right to be authoritative to them or to anybody else. James concluded that one must be critical about the kind of revelations that mystics experience without undermining their capacity to receive or express them.

On the other hand, James rejected the criterion of rational consciousness based upon the understanding and the senses alone because they represent only one possible type of consciousness. Having said that, James's pragmatism goes beyond the materialist-scientific view that postulates that one can only formulate theories that are empirically demonstrable by sense-perception alone. Therefore, James left open the possibility of interpreting the mystical phenomena using other methods in the scientific study of religion.

St. John of the Cross, three centuries earlier, did recognize some of the mystical marks or characteristics described by William James in *The Varieties of Religious Experience*. The effects of mystical or contemplative union with the divine, John says, are: "an elevation of the mind to heavenly knowledge and a withdrawal and abstraction from all objects, forms, and figures and from the remembrance of them."[45]

Of course, John states that the contemplative experience is of "short duration."[46] It is ineffable because it "cannot be caught in words."[47] Nor can it be explained adequately. It is passive because the human intellect and all the other faculties are grasped or held by a power greater than themselves receiving revelations or secret wisdom from God "without any effort of its own."[48] Similarly, in James's words, the mystic has gained direct access to supreme knowledge because the experience in itself has a noetic quality as a result of an encounter with the divine who teaches a lofty, sublime

---

[45] John of the Cross, *The Collected Works*, 195; *Ascent* 2.14.11.

[46] Ibid.

[47] Ibid., 470; *Spiritual Canticle*, Prologue, 1.

[48] Ibid., 531; *Spiritual Canticle* 14-15.14.

science to the blessed soul. John affirms that God "supernaturally instructs in his divine wisdom the soul that is empty and unhindered."[49]

But in what sense could John be viewed as a prophet? John could have easily followed Thomas Merton's definition of the prophet not as "one who predicts future events" but rather "in a more traditional sense of one who 'utters' and 'announces' news about man's own deepest trouble." [50]

John uses the definition of prophecy in two ways. On the one hand, the prophet is one who listens to the Word of God; and thus receives a message from God, that is, a divine revelation. John asks, "[w]hom will God instruct? And to whom will he explain his word and prophecy?"[51] On the other hand, the prophet is one who bears witness to truth, justice, and love (or charity). John quotes St. Paul to support his second definition of prophecy in the following passage:

> *If I speak in human and angelic tongues and do not have charity, I am like a sounding metal or bell. And if I have prophecy and know all mysteries and all knowledge, and if I have all of faith so as to move mountains, and do not have charity, I am nothing, and so on [1 Cor. 13:1-2]. When those who esteem their works in this way seek glory from Christ saying: Lord, did we not prophesy in your name and work many miracles? He will answer: Depart from me, workers of iniquity [Mt. 7:22-23].*[52]

Also, John is fond of quoting biblical passages from Exodus, especially those dealing with the Hebrew prophet, Moses. John writes: "After the 400 years in which the children of Israel had been afflicted by their slavery in Egypt, God declared to Moses: I have seen the affliction of my people and

---

[49] Ibid., 387; *Dark Night* 1.12.4.

[50] Thomas Merton, *The Literary Essays of Thomas Merton*, ed. Patrick Hart (New York: New Directions, 1985), 3.

[51] John of the Cross, *The Collected Works*, 215; *Ascent* 2.19.6.

[52] Ibid., 324; *Ascent* 3.30.4.

have come down to free them [Ex. 3:7-8], even though he had always seen it."⁵³

Let me pause for a moment and ruminate upon those words. John declares that God has seen the affliction of the Jewish people. But why did not God act in a timely manner to put a stop to the unneeded affliction? Was the suffering of the Jewish people necessary? Or could it be said that God is in need of humans so that human beings can build the heavenly kingdom on earth by becoming co-creators? I believe John would admit that God is against all social injustices in the world; that suffering sometimes is inevitable, but not necessary (similarly to what Buddhists think when they say "pain is inevitable but suffering is optional"); and finally, that God is calling humans to participate as co-creators in building the kingdom of God on earth by denouncing the deepest troubles of humanity and by announcing the good news of a new reality, a new order, that definitely put a stop to the affliction and unnecessary suffering of the *anawim*.

John's ascetico-mystical teachings are not designed to cause pain and anguish to the human soul as an end in themselves. On the contrary, John's major task is precisely to free the soul from all personal and societal obstacles that impede union with God. Nevertheless, a human soul cannot feel totally free without experiencing some degree of pain and suffering in this life. Pain and suffering are an integral part of life. Otherwise human beings would not be able to grow. This could explain why John spoke so tenderly about his trials and afflictions. As he puts it in the *Sayings of Light and Love*, "Have great love for trials and think of them as but a small way of pleasing your Bridegroom, who did not hesitate to die for you."⁵⁴

John understands that prophesy, in the sense of mystical revelations, must go hand in hand with the second definition of prophesy in the sense of

---

⁵³ Ibid., 488; *Spiritual Canticle* 2.4.

⁵⁴ Ibid., 92; John's saying is catalogued as number 94.

serving God with true love, "for in charity lies the fruit of eternal life."[55] As Peter Henriot points out:

> *"Faith without works is dead." This is the blunt answer given by the Apostle James to the perennial question about the relationship between belief and deeds. Today, we might phrase the question differently. We might ask about the relationship between faith and justice, prayer and action, spirituality and social commitment. But the answer is still the same. Faith without works is dead.*[56]

The question then becomes: Can the mystic still feel the divine presence within and around without fully committing himself or herself to a life of service for God? Is John's faith alive without the works of peace, justice and charity? Conversely, is John's faith alive with the pursuit of social and religious justice? Clearly John embraces the two definitions of prophecy in his writings. He says:

The prophets, entrusted with the word of God, were well aware of this. Prophecy for them was a severe trial because, as we affirmed, the people observed that a good portion of the prophecy did not come about in accord with the letter of what was said to them. As a result, the people laughed at the prophets and made much fun of them. It reached such a point that Jeremiah exclaimed: They mock me all day long, everyone scoffs at and despises me because for a long time now I have cried out against iniquity and promised them destruction, and the Lord's word has become a reproach to me and a mockery all the time. And I said: I do not have to remember him or speak any more in his name [Jer. 20:7-9].[57]

Like the ancient prophets, John endured suffering. It is not shocking at all to find out that John was persecuted in his own time by inquisitors and by a few of his own Carmelite brothers. According to John's foes, he was

---

[55] Ibid., 324; *Ascent* 3.30.5.

[56] Katherine Marie Dyckman and L. Patrick Carroll, *Inviting the Mystic, Supporting the Prophet: An Introduction to Spiritual Direction* (New York: Paulist Press, 1981), ix.

[57] John of the Cross, *The Collected Works*, 222; *Ascent* 2.20.6.

holding unorthodox Christian ideas and practices. He was accused of being an illuminist and a quietist. In sixteenth century Spain, mysticism was not welcomed in some religious circles.

His foes were suspicious of new religious movements mainly composed of lay people, Jewish and Moorish converts, and Lutherans, because most of them rejected the position of the Catholic Church in matters of faith, salvation, sin, and sacraments. Some religious figures (like Miguel de Molinos) believed that the human soul can find salvation without the mediation of the Catholic Church, meaning that humans do not need to confess before a priest, or receive certain sacraments, and so forth, because eventually God's grace alone will save the human soul.

John sided with those who suffered in his own time, especially the Carmelite nuns and Father Gracián. John announced the deepest troubles of his Carmelite brothers and sisters. And because of that political friction within the Carmeilte order, he suffered persecution at the hands of some his own Carmelite brothers. He was mocked and humiliated, put in prison for nine months, forced to leave his administrative offices, and sent to La Peñuela as a forced exile.

And as I pointed out earlier the most probable *converso* lineage in John could have been reason enough to be mistreated, denounced to the Holy Inquisition, and being marginalized within his own Carmelite order and within the Spanish society in their quest for a new religious and political order based on purity of blood laws that require anyone living in the Peninsula to follow only the true Catholic faith. As their motto says, convert or perish.

 Why did John get into so much trouble? Why was John forced to quit his administrative positions within the Carmelite Order? Why did Doria want John to leave the Iberian Peninsula? Could it be viewed as an attempt to get rid of John by sending him to Mexico and thus removing him from the religious order? The plan never took place because John died in Úbeda before embarking with other Carmelites to the new world. But it is known today that some Carmelites working for Doria took the necessary steps to remove John of his Carmelite habit. As William Barnstone notes:

> he [John] was stripped of all office and exiled to la Peñuela, a desert house in Andalusia. Evidence was collected against him, some of it tragi-comic, such as a false accusation by a nun in Málaga that she had been kissed by Fray Juan through the grille of her window. At Beas de Segura, his favorite convent, the nuns destroyed all papers and letters from him, for fear of being implicated with the heretic monk. There was a move to expel him from the order, and only his sickness spared him this last step.[58]

John stood against Doria's efforts of centralizing the Discalced Carmelite Order, which left the nuns at his mercy, even at the expense of losing all his power within the Carmelite Order. John, the co-adjutor and co-founder of the Discalced Carmelite friars and a loyal friend to the Teresian reform, was released by Doria's decree of all his office duties before he died. John was sent to the hermitage of la Peñuela, away from the new Council formed by Doria. John was definitely a mystical prophet, not the simple rebel as he was often accused of being.

John faced the martyrdom of rejection by his own Carmelite brothers. He paid the price of aligning himself with those who were oppressed. Like Jesus, he suffered persecution. And perhaps his death was linked to his enemies' constant oppression for being a *converso*. Peter Slattery correctly understood John's prophetic role when he wrote:

> St. John, the poet, being a person of discernment, was sensitive to the injustices and exaggerations of his time, and in his innocence he made people aware of them. Poets are uncomfortable people to be with. Certainly, toward the end of his life those with power did not want him close to them. St. John, the poet, called on his fellow religious to examine stagnation in their lives and institutions--he did this by the force of the sanctity of his life and the power of his poetry. He was a silent

---

[58]Willis Barnstone, *The Poems of Saint John of the Cross* (New York: A New Directions Book, 1972), 17.

contemplative who suffered, not only because of his own empathy, but because he threatened the powerful. Out of his silence he caressed and challenged all who read his poetry.[59]

The history of constant persecutions bears witness to the prophetic dimension of St. John of the Cross. Also, it could explain John's apparent silence concerning social justice issues. He, like the ancient prophets, aligned himself with the oppressed (in that case, with the nuns, but John also stood behind the moderate Carmelite, Gracián, who was ultimately expelled from the Order), suffering persecution and perhaps martyrdom. I will later explain in more detail the historical circumstances and the theological implications of such events.

Ultimately, I share Janet Ruffing's and Karl Rahner's observations on the historical misjudgment by theologians that the contemplative life is superior to the active life when they say:

> *It is no accident that the prophetic and the mystical have been systematically separated from one another. Karl Rahner claims: it can be said with but little exaggeration that the history of mystical theology is a history of the devaluation of the prophetic element in favor of the non-prophetic, "pure" infused contemplation. People are more suspicious of prophetic mysticism, which invokes revelations and instructions from above to claim a mission and right in the Church to admonish and guide the Church and her members, than of the image-free, ineffable mysticism of pure contemplation. Certainly, the former is more dangerous and prone to come into conflict with Church authority than the latter.*[60]

---

[59]Slattery, *The Springs of Carmel*, 74.

[60] Janet Ruffing, "Introduction," in *Mysticism & Social Transformation*, 8-9.

2

THE LIFE & WRITINGS
OF SAINT JOHN OF THE CROSS

There are certain challenges in studying and researching St. John of the Cross. This study cannot limit its scope to just reading his poetry or mystical theology without examining other important aspects of his life and thoughts that have been ignored or overlooked for so long. A more balanced picture of the Carmelite saint is needed, in order to reveal his true character.

The purpose of this chapter is to review some of the major events in the life of St. John of the Cross so that some of the misinterpretations mentioned earlier in the introduction of this study can be analyzed. This chapter will demonstrate the important role that John played as a contemplative in action.

I will present in this chapter sufficient evidence to prove how active John was in his own time through his apostolic service in and outside the monastic life by way of teaching, preaching, and engaging in other activities such as funding new convents, serving the community, healing the sick, administering the sacraments, building aqueducts, partaking of civic or administrative duties, and so on. All in all, John's actions spring from his contemplative vision, which is firmly rooted in his theology of love.

The lack of references in John's writings to the historical events and the social environment in which he lived may be not his fault but rather the result of circumstances apart from him. The problem of *conversos* could partly explain John's apparent silence. Again, John lived in a period of time when the kingdom of Castile promulgated the code of "*pureza de sangre*" (purity of blood), an age that St. Teresa of Ávila used to call, in Castilian, "*tiempos recios*" (harsh times). In such an intolerant age when Spanish inquisitors are allowed to persecute in the name of God those who do not practice the Catholic faith, it makes sense to say that Jewish and Moorish *conversos* would not say much about their lineage.

If John was a new Christian, this alone would have explained his fear of speaking his mind about some of the most acute social and religious problems of his time. This alone should suffice to explain why neither John nor Teresa could speak about their own blood lineage. They will be sent immediately to the *Santo Oficio*, as in fact we know it happened since there were some attempts to denounce the two of them to the Spanish inquisitors. They never were found guilty, but the suspicion was always present in the eyes of their enemies.

One must also remember that John's monastic upbringing had a great influence on his apparent silence due to the perceived role of the monk in the world. Furthermore, John took the vows of silence, poverty, obedience, and chastity, as his religious order prescribed in the rules of St. Albert. Without doubt, the religious friar was allowed to write about contemplation and the life of prayer, but he knew how difficult it would be for him to write about social issues, especially under such harsh inquisitorial times.

John, who was probably born in a new Christian family, of Jewish and of Moorish *converso* stock, wrote his prose commentaries, poems, counsels, and letters under great pressure. He would have feared being persecuted by the inquisitors and would have been subjected to constant censorship by his own Carmelite brothers. John was surely aware of the risks people took in his time, especially after seeing how Friar Luis de León, one of the most popular professors in the University of Salamanca, was arrested and imprisoned for several years. The historical reason for Luis's imprisonment was his translation from the Hebrew Scriptures of the *Song of Solomon* (or most commonly known in the Christian mystical tradition as the *Song of Songs*).

But modern scholars have shed some new light on Friar Luis's Jewish *converso* background. As a matter of fact, we now know that Friar Luis was the one in charge of editing the whole collection of writings by Teresa of Ávila, and his nephew Fray Basilio Ponce de León defended John of the Cross posthumously after the Inquisition was investigating John's works for being heretical. This proves there was a direct link and connection between all these great Spanish writers of descendant of *converso* families who were more inclined to form a network of friends to support each other under such harsh times in sixteenth century Spain.

That was in the case of Miguel de Cervantes y Saavedra (1547-1616), who was another descendant of Jewish *conversos* and whose sister entered to profess the vows of becoming a nun under the Discalced Carmelites in Alcalá de Henares. After visiting myself the house of Cervantes in Alcalá de Henares, it is obvious that his home was part of the old *judería*, or the Jewish neighborhood.

For all of these *converso* families, it was a matter of survival to be associated with the right group of people in order to avoid persecutions. We have seen that reality later corroborated in the twentieth century under the Nazi persecution of the Jews in Europe.

Edith Stein the famous Carmelite religious sister and philosopher is a good modern example of these persecutions. Even after Edith has converted to the Catholic faith, the Nazis arrested her and sent her and many others to the Auschwitz concentration camp where she died in the gas chamber on August 9, 1942. Incidentally, Edith adopted the religious names of both co-founders of the Discalced Carmelite tradition naming herself Teresa Benedict of the Cross and wrote a famous book titled *The Science of the Cross*, dedicated to the study of John's mystical theology.

In sixteenth century Castile, the Catholic Church still maintained Latin as her official language. As a result of this mandate, those who broke away from the Latin tradition were seen as outsiders. The unorthodox and the heretic posed a direct threat to the status quo and to the religious authority of the Catholic Church.

In an age of Protestant heresies and the invention of the printing-press, Christian believers gained more access to the biblical texts using the vernacular language. As a result, Protestant reformers and theologians allowed every single Christian to interpret the Bible according to his or her state of perfection, holding the principle of the priesthood of all believers. This is why many *iluminados* and *alumbrados* were heavily persecuted in the Iberian Peninsua by the Dominican inquisitors, and among them we find the names of Teresa and John being reported to the *Santo Oficio*.

Without doubt, these new religious movements affected the hierarchy of the Roman Catholic Church. Protestant Christians were no longer in need of priests or Popes serving as mediators between God and their souls. By that time, Protestant mystics claimed that they had gained a direct, immediate access to the divine world without priestly intervention. They read the Bible alone as their only source of authority, because by God's grace they were anointed with the gift of divine prophecy and divine revelation. From then onwards, Christians would read the biblical texts in their vernacular languages with or without the magisterial interpretation of the Church.

Protestant Christians, heretics, and unorthodox Christians alike were under the constant scrutiny of religious inquisitors. Again, if John was a new Christian, that alone could get him into serious problems with the Spanish Inquisition. Furthermore, John instructed lay and religious people, thereby giving them the opportunity to read biblical texts and learn about different theological views in the language of Cervantes. Indeed, John's writings are full of allusions to the Bible and to different schools of thought from Platonism to Thomism. He probably knew the risks involved by undertaking such enterprises. But life would be meaningless without devoting oneself to that which he or she firmly believes in.

As a scholar, John gained some reputation in university centers, especially when he became the rector of the Carmelite houses of study in Alcalá and Baeza. But he was probably better known as a great spiritual director within the Discalced Carmelite tradition. This historical awareness of John's intellectual environment presses us to develop a hermeneutics of suspicion that will attempt to expose the powerful forces behind the systematic distortions that John's life and works could have suffered from.

Juan de Yepes y Álvarez was his secular name, son of Gonzalo de Yepes and Catalina Álvarez, and the youngest of three sons. John was born in Fontiveros (Ávila), at the heart of the Castilian region known as la Moraña. This region was heavily populated by Moorish converts, or in Spanish, *moriscos*. There are some disputes about the right date of his birth. Some scholars believe that John was born around June 24, 1540. However, the most accepted year among SanJuanist scholars is 1542 due to the age recorded as 49 at the time of his death, on December 14, 1591.

Some commentators have stressed the importance of aristocratic or noble lineage in John's blood. Nonetheless, this is far from being demonstrated, in spite of those who took for granted John's noble lineage. The story goes that Gonzalo's family, who were silk merchants in Toledo (a trade that usually belonged to Jewish *converso* families), disinherited John's father from their wealth for getting married to Catalina, a poor young woman who could also have inherited the social stigma of having been born into a Moorish family.

This event in John's life is significant because if it is true, it could prove how close John was to the Muslim world (especially to the Sufi mystical tradition). Luce López Baralt the famous scholar from Puerto Rico, has done an intensive study on John's poetry and commentaries and has concluded that John's mystical poetry share many symbols with the Sufi language of the dark night and intoxicated love.[1]

Furthermore, it is not a pure coincidence that John spent many years living in Andalusia, especially seven years of his mature life where spent in Granada where he became the prior of Los Mártires, where he was inspired to write many of his poems and commentaries just a few steps from the Alhambra palace, the last bastion of the Muslims in Spain.

Even after the expulsion of the Moors from Granada there were many *moriscos* who were allowed to stay there if they live as good Catholics. In the mid-half of sixteenth century Spain, many of these *moriscos* lived in the famous neighborhood of El Albaicín, and some escaped to live in las Alpujarras where they enjoyed more freedom from being persecuted by old Christians. Many of these *moriscos* clung to practice Islam in secret, so by the time John arrived in Granada there was still a palpable Moorish presence of Al-Andalus in south of Spain.

In one of my trips to Granada, I found *mudéjar* inscriptions in the large aqueduct that John built with the help of his brother Francisco that still sits in the hills of el Carmen de los Mártires. Are these combinations of Christian and Moorish art part of the Andalusian region of Granada? Why would a Christian monk design his aqueduct with these Moorish influences? Is this part of another clue to understanding his *converso* legacy, left to us as an unfinished puzzle through the thousands of kilometers that he walked in his lifetime between Spain and Portugal?

John's mother moved the family to Arévalo when she was widowed in 1545. Gonzalo's extended family rejected him, while he was still alive, for having married Catalina, a poor woman (again, perhaps a Moorish *converso*). Even after his death, they did not offer Catalina's family much help, forcing her to support her three sons alone. In 1547, Luis, one of John's older brothers, died as a result of years of malnutrition and economic

---

[1] Luce López Baralt, *Asedios a lo Indecible: San Juan de la Cruz canta al éxtasis transformante* (Madrid: Editorial Trotta, 1998) 17-18.

penury. John's lifetime health problems can also be traced to those early years of living poorly under such extreme economic conditions.

Poverty and deprivation definitively marked John's early years, but love reigned in his family. It is well documented that his parents got married because they truly loved each other, even at the expense of Gonzalo being disinherited from his wealthy family. This event shows how rare and exceptional John's family was at a time when marriages were arranged by families according to their social caste system. The troubles of the Yepes y Álvarez family prepared little John for the numerous challenges that he would face later in his life.

Arévalo did not meet their economic expectations and social needs. In 1551, Catalina's family moved to Medina del Campo, a market town heavily populated by Jewish and Muslim *conversos*. Medina del Campo attracted people from all over Europe to its international fairs. Famous for their trade skills, the well-organized Jewish *converso* community gave Medina del Campo an unprecedented economic boom.

Catalina worked as a weaver, a typical profession held by new Christian descendants of *moriscos*. John's older brother, Francisco, helped her, bringing some money to the household. Medina del Campo became the real home for Catalina and her family. She spent the rest of her life living close to the Carmelite convent. The nuns took great care of her before she died, and she is buried there in a Discalced Carmelite convent.

John loved studying. In sixteenth century Spain, education was seen as a dangerous thing. Many Jewish *converso* families stressed the importance of learning and studying. However, they were under the constant vigilance of the Spanish inquisitors. It is no surprise that John became an altar boy. This religious event in John's early life might have erased any serious suspicion from the inquisitors, if and only if he was a descendant of a *converso* family. Or perhaps, it might have been conducive to proving that new Christians had embraced the Catholic faith.

In Medina del Campo, John attended the Catechism school at the *Colegio de la doctrina*. This elementary school was dedicated to the education of poor children, notably orphans and sons of new Christians. They were carefully instructed in the Catholic doctrine and some had the opportunity to become apprentices in trades. This is similar to what we saw in North America when Native Americans were forcibly converted by Christian missionaries and sent to Christian boarding schools to learn the language, the culture and the faith. All of them were heavily indoctrinated and inculturated under the Spanish Catholic empire and later under the Anglo-American dominion to the Western territories that extended all the way to California where the Spanish missions were located.

As John grew up, he worked as an apprentice at various trades such as carpentry, tailoring, wood-carving, and painting. Some commentators report that John "showed no enthusiasm"[2] at those trades. However, it is well known that John used those acquired skills as a Carmelite reformer when he undertook such tasks as designing, building, and decorating new monasteries and convents.

John also served as an acolyte at the Church of la Magdalena between 1551 and 1555. He had to assist in the sacristy for several hours each day, and he was sent to collect alms for the church. This office helped him to be recruited at the Hospital of Las Bubas. He raised funds for the hospital, a center dedicated to patients infected with venereal diseases. He worked there until 1563, under the tutelage of his protector, Don Alonso Álvarez de Toledo, who was the administrator of the hospital.

During his years working at the hospital, John learned how to cultivate the virtue of compassion by being confronted on a daily basis with such harsh realities as the pain, suffering, and death of his patients. Nonetheless, there have been numerous reports of how John quickly put into practice his early years of experience working in the hospital. John took personal care of those who fell ill in the monasteries while he was the prior in

---

[2] John of the Cross, *The Collected Works*, 10.

Granada. He fed them by preparing delicious food with the best ingredients available at the monastery. Also, he told them stories and jokes, or recited poems to uplift the spirits of the ill. In short, John's treatment was humanitarian; his austere and pious image in the past didn't capture the real compassionate person behind the monastic walls.

Between 1555 and 1560 John studied humanities in a Jesuit education center in Medina, while he was working in the hospital. Don Alonso gave John the opportunity to study at a Jesuit school, thinking that once he finished his studies he could offer him the position of the chaplain for the hospital. John studied under the tutelage of one of the best educators of his time, Father Bonifacio. He would have taken courses in grammar, rhetoric, history, Latin, Greek, and perhaps arts or philosophy. These courses helped him gain the knowledge and discipline to become, much later, one of the best Spanish writers and poets in the history of Spanish literature.

Literary critics (Dámaso Alonso, Jorgue Guillén, Gerald Brenan, Colin Thompson), philosophers (Jean Baruzi, Henri Bergson, Jacques Maritain, Daniel Dombrowski, Blair Reynolds), theologians (William Johnston, Miguel Asín Palacios, Petter Slattery, Gustavo Gutiérrez, Segundo Galilea, David Perrin, James Arraj) from all over the world have praised John's poetry and his own creativity as a thinker. In mixing different literary styles and intellectual sources, John helped to enhance the Castilian language by bringing old and new elements together into the Spanish grammar, and also by incorporating a vast knowledge accumulated through his years as a student and friar.

After graduation, John had the option to stay at the hospital working as a chaplain. But could he have become a chaplain without first having been ordained as a priest? Some commentators, like José Vicente Rodríguez, suggested that perhaps John studied more courses than those listed above. He could have also received some training in the Carmelite house of Santa Ana, including the study of philosophy and theology.

In 1563, John decided to enter the Strict Observant (or Calced) Carmelite Order in Medina del Campo where he lived as a novice friar. John's unexpected choice of entering the Carmelite Order could easily be explained if it is true that he received formal training in Medina del Campo before being accepted as a friar. He adopted the religious name of Friar John of St. Matthias, or in Spanish, Fray Juan de Santo Matía. (Some scholars have wrongly translated the Spanish name as Saint Matthew.)

In 1564, John was sent by the Calced Carmelites to study at the College of Saint Andrew at Salamanca, where he attended three years in the arts program and one year in theology. The arts program in his time corresponds to our study in humanities today. Salamanca was one of the most prestigious intellectual centers in Europe after Bologna, Oxford, and Paris. Studying there allowed John to take courses with some of the most well-known professors of his time.

In the words of Keith J. Egan,

> *Basically, John of the Cross is in the Augustinian tradition and a Platonist. One example of John's Augustinian affiliation is his use of the three faculties of the soul, intellect, will and memory rather than the Thomist rendition of intellect and will as the soul's spiritual faculties ... To make John of the Cross a through-going Thomist puts his teaching in a context not faithful to his vision of the contemplative life. John was much more at home in the Platonic tradition.*[3]

A contemporary of John was the famous Augustinian theologian Friar Luis de León, who taught theology courses at the University of Salamanca. It was Friar Luis, also a Jewish *converso*, who edited the collected works of St. Teresa of Ávila, and it was his nephew Fray Basilio Ponce de León the one who "used the works of the Victorines to defend Fray Juan when his works were under investigation by the Inquisition."[4] Ironically, a

---

[3] Keith J. Egan, "Thomas Merton's Approach to St. John of the Cross," in *The Merton Annual: Studies in Culture, Spirituality and Social Concerns* Volume 20, ed. Victor A. Kramer (Louisville: Fons Vitae, 2007) 68.

[4] R. A. Herrera, *Silent Music: The Life, Work, and Thought of St. John of the Cross* (Grand Rapids, Michigan: William B. Eermans Publishing Company, 2004) 38.

descendent of a Jewish *converso* defended John against posthumous accusations of heresy.

Other professors who taught courses at the University of Salamanca during John's four years of study were Francisco de Vitoria, Domingo and Pedro de Soto, Melchor Cano, Bartolomé Medina, Mancio de Corpus Christi, and Domingo Báñez. Without doubt, John received a superb education in Salamanca, learning from an array of schools of thought from Augustinianism to Thomism to Scotism.

John's writings were eclectic, incorporating ideas from the diverse sources to which he had been exposed over the course of his life. As a good mystic John absorbed all the great wisdom and teachings that were present in his day and he interpreted his mystical experiences using different schools of thought and sources coming from different faith traditions from the pagan traditions of Plato, Aristotle, Plotinus, and the Stoics to the study of Jewish, Christian and Muslim thinkers who most probably he has studied in Salamanca. As we know later in his life John encountered people from all walks of life in his numerous trips throughout Spain and Portugal, including visiting many university cities where *conversos* live.

At the same time, John received religious training at the Carmelite house of San Andrés. This house of studies opened in 1480 offering religious students a place to live the Carmelite life while they studied philosophy and theology in the university. Thus, John was trained in the intellectual and spiritual formation of the fourteenth century Carmelite masters, especially the English John Baconthorp and the Italian Miguel de Bolonia. Also, John's years of training in Salamanca helped him acquire a vast knowledge of the Christian mystical tradition which he used as the foundation of his theological and mystical commentaries and poems.

John had great success in his scholastic and religious studies in Salamanca. In 1567, he was appointed prefect of studies. This position was granted to only the most talented students. It entailed teaching some classes daily, defending public theses, and resolving academic exercises raised by the professor. No wonder Teresa later called John "my little Seneca."

A Roman philosopher born in Spain and influenced by the Stoic school, Seneca was regarded as one of the best minds that the Iberian Peninsula ever witnessed. Some suggested that John was a sort of Stoic thinker. SanJuanist commentators found some parallels between John's thoughts and the Stoics', especially in their philosophy of the middle way, on how to avoid extremes and maintain the proper balance in life.

While John was finishing his studies in Salamanca, he was ordained a priest. In 1567, John said his first Mass in Medina del Campo, where at the age of twenty-five he met with St. Teresa of Ávila, who was twice his age. They spoke about their projects and dreams. He heard about the Teresian reform and Teresa's plan of organizing her second religious foundation in Medina. Teresa asked permission to Father Rubeo to get licenses for the new foundation of Discalced Carmelite monasteries for friars. She was looking for the right people to lead this new counter-reform movement.

Why did John want to leave the Calced Carmelite Order? Why would he take the risk of leaving an already established monastic order? The story goes that John suffered a crisis as a university student. He was searching for a contemplative order. He even thought about leaving the Calced Carmelite Order and becoming a member of the Carthusian monastic tradition, which was one of the most contemplative orders of his time. After his meeting with Teresa, he decided to stay in the Carmelite Order. But now he changed his Calced Carmelite habit for the Discalced one. Teresa's reform was officially approved but restricted to building new nuns' convents. Even so, she probably knew at some point that the ecclesiastical authorities would let her build a Discalced Carmelite friary.

It is difficult to know the reasons why John entered the Carmelite Order and then adopted the Discalced Carmelite habit. It is easy to assume that John felt at home with Teresa and the Teresian reform. Why? Was John a *converso* like her? Both Teresa and John were born in the province of Ávila, which was at that time part of the old kingdom of Castile and Aragon. Juan de Yepes y Álvarez was born between 1540 and 1542 in Fontiveros, a rural village in the province of Ávila, located approximately 25 miles from the capital. Teresa de Cepeda y Ahumada was born in Gotarrendura (Ávila) on 28 March 1515.

Sixteenth century Castilians became obsessed with the new promulgated code of purity of blood, a code that unsuccessfully attempted to track down individuals who did not belong to old Christian families. The apparent purpose of this code of honor was to preserve their identity as Christians by avoiding any possible threat of mixing with the Jewish or Muslim *converso* population.

Old Christians built a network of suspicion and distrust against anyone who could not prove their Christian lineage. This is why the Church used the institution of the Holy Inquisition. The Church, with the help of the civil authorities, persecuted those who practiced in secret Judaism, Islam, Lutheranism, or any other faith distinct from the Old Christians.

But the fact of the matter is that, behind this climate of religious intolerance, there were other reasons hidden from the public, based on economic and political plans for the new vision of the Iberian Peninsula. For instance, it is historically well known how the Church, with the help of civil authorities, confiscated the properties of those who were persecuted in the name of the one and only true faith.

Sociologically, both Teresa's and John's families lived under great pressure because of their *converso* origins. In John's case, as noted, it is very possible that he had not only Jewish but also Moorish blood. They both were forced by their historical circumstances to establish a noble status and a safe refuge in the monastic life. Purity and honor ruled Teresa's and John's social world.

Religiously, Teresa and John, like all members of *converso* families, had to show more than anyone else that they were zealous Catholic practitioners. They might have converted because of their deep belief in the new faith, but something remains to be said: the social pressure of the time forced large number of Jews and Muslims to adopt the Christian faith. In my view, there are so many connections to people, places, and stories

impregnated with Jewish and Moorish flavors that it is shortsighted to disregard the evidence when it is in front of us.

Jews settled down in Spain by the first century after the second destruction of the Jewish temple in Jerusalem. According to some scholars they moved to Spain via Phoenicians, who were the famous merchants of the sea, and they landed in Hispania, which was by then a Roman province.

In the case of Muslims, they arrive in Spain in 711 through their incursions in the Strait of Gibraltar. Even after the expulsions of Jews in 1492 and Muslims in 1616, many of their descendants spent many centuries living in the Iberian Peninsula, and they were as Spanish by birth as anyone else.

Being born myself in Ceuta, Spain and after following the footsteps of the Carmelite mystics in the Iberian Peninsula I have no doubt in my mind that John like Teresa was of *converso* origins. This would explain why they both faced so many trials and tribulations while they were alive, and why their writings share some similarities with the Jewish cabalistic themes and the Sufi imagery.

At the age of seven, Teresa ran away with her elder brother Rodrigo to "the land of the Moors" in search of martyrdom. Could this incident be seen as an example of being overwhelmed by the social pressure of Teresa's environment? Why did Teresa's older brothers later emigrate to the Indies to convert the native inhabitants into the Christian faith? Why did her brothers seek fame and fortune? Perhaps, the Cepedas y Ahumadas were trying to erase any suspicion of being descendants of Jews by becoming *hidalgos*; that is to say, those people whose families were of noble birth. Without notifying her father, Teresa decided to join a convent, breaking with the traditional view in her home that a woman should be married soon and serve her husband.

Teresa's parents were don Alonso Sánchez de Cepeda (from Toledo), a tax-gatherer, and doña Beatriz de Ahumada (from Olmedo). The family might well have belonged to the social caste of "*hidalgos*," and until recently, Teresa's family was regarded as one of the purest noble families of

Castile. However, in 1948, Teresian scholar Narciso Alonso Cortés uncovered a lawsuit brought against her paternal grandfather, Juan Sánchez de Cepeda, which demonstrated her Jewish *converso* stock. Cortés found the lawsuit in the Archives of the Royal Chancellery of Valladolid.

In 1485, Teresa's grandfather confessed publicly to the crime of reversion, of being guilty of apostasy; that is to say, of practicing Judaism in secret. As Carol Lee Flinders narrates:

> *[Juan Sánchez and his children] marched through the streets of the city in penitential procession, dressed in yellow garments marked with black crosses, visiting all the cathedrals in turn while the citizens of the town threw stones, spat, and cursed them--not just once, and not twice, but every Friday for seven weeks.*[5]

The Tribunal of the Inquisition did offer a pardon to all those who confessed their secret practices. Juan Sánchez de Cepeda, his wife, and his sons (including Teresa's father, Alonso) were reconciled to the church in an *auto de fe* that required them to wear the infamous yellow *sambenitos con sus cruces* on seven successive Fridays and to walk barefoot through the streets of Toledo. The *sambenito*, a garment painted with flames and devils was worn to the stake, marked with black crosses. The *sambenitos* were inscribed later in the parish churches with the disgraced families' names.

Teresa's grandfather had been socially accepted again in Toledo after doing public penance. But the integrity and dignity of the family suffered irreparably, especially after enduring great humiliation. They were always looked at with suspicion by the Castilian inquisitors who "operated under the certainty that *conversos* were particularly vulnerable to heresy and demonic possession."[6] *Conversos* or *marranos* (pigs), as they were often called, had no other alternative than to conform to the dominant culture in order to survive.

---

[5] Carol Lee Flinders, *Enduring Grace (San Francisco:* HarperSanFrancisco, 1993), 159.

[6] Ibid., 160.

Alonso's family moved not long after to live in Ciudad Real, where Juan Sánchez changed their family name to Cepeda, and later decided to change residence to Ávila, "a city known for its proudly held tradition of religious tolerance."[7] Nevertheless, the citizens of Ávila started to become suspicious of those who came from Toledo and other towns known for their numerous Jewish and Muslim *converso* inhabitants. Both Teresa's and John's families came from Toledo and from Yepes (located in the province of Toledo).

Could it be possible that their families already knew each other from those early years living in the small province of Toledo? This is the theory proposed by José Gómez-Menor Fuentes, which, if true, would very well explain both John's decision to enter the Discalced Carmelite Order and his close friendship with Teresa. Gómez-Menor declares: "Por otra partida del mismo libro se llega a la certeza de que el nombre completo del padrino es Alonso Alvarez de Fuensalida, el cual estaba casado, como vimos, con una Cepeda. Parientes de san Juan de la Cruz y de santa Teresa se conocían muy bien."[8]

Both Teresa's and John's families acquired a socially esteemed lineage after they amassed little fortunes. Their families held the typical professions of *conversos* (silk merchants, tax-collectors) in their time. Sixteenth century Castile's codes of purity of blood excluded all *conversos* from many levels of society. Jewish converts exteriorly acted as new Christians, although some continued to practice Judaism in the attics of their homes, hidden from the rest of society. However, many Jewish families deliberately forgot their roots. They even denounced other Jewish families for practicing Judaism in secret. These harsh historical circumstances could explain why

---

[7] Ibid.

[8] José Gómez-Menor Fuentes, *El linaje familiar de santa Teresa y de san Juan de la Cruz: Sus parientes toledanos* (Toledo, Spain: Gráficas Cervantes, 1970), 44. The English version reads: "Through another birth certificate from the same book we know with certainty that the full name of the godfather is Alonso Alvarez de Fuensalida, who was married, as we saw, with a Cepeda. Relatives of saint John of the Cross and Saint Teresa knew each other very well [my own translation]."

Teresa's and John's social backgrounds were not mentioned in their writings. I am convinced that they did deliberately omit any public reference to their family's backgrounds for fear of being persecuted.

Earlier hagiographers could have overlooked the social background of "the Sephardic Mother" for two main reasons: 1) they truly lacked knowledge of her social background, which I seriously doubt; or 2) they falsified the documents in order to avoid further persecutions since any direct evidence of Jewish blood found in the Carmelite foundress could be fatal to the Discalced Carmelite reform. According to Efrén de la Madre de Dios and Otger Steggink, the Church suppressed the Jewish element in Teresa for fear of scandalizing their readers.[9]

This fear of being denounced to the Inquisition could have explained both Teresa's and John's apparent silence about their *converso* stock. Teresa's family did purchase a certificate of *hidalguía*, the lowest rank of nobility in the aristocratic lineage, which could only be used in the three places where they were residents, Ávila, Hortigosa and Manjabálago. Her family had to move from Toledo, the old Jewish capital of Europe, to Ávila, where the noble families were settled. Teresa's grandfather had secured his family position in the community, but not without paying a high price. The next generations of the Cepedas further secured their social position by military appointments, by New World conquests in the Americas, by marrying into noble families, and by entering into religious orders: not only Teresa but many of her relatives entered the Discalced Carmelite Order. Jesuits and Carmelites did not require the codes of purity of blood until the end of the sixteenth century.

It is not pure coincidence that a great number of Jewish and Moorish *conversos*, among them nuns, monks, priests, lay people and mystics, entered the Jesuit and Carmelite Orders seeking refuge and personal growth. Francisco Márquez Villanueva, in *Espiritualidad y Literatura en el Siglo XVI*, proved Américo Castro's theory, in *España en su historia*, that the Teresian

---

[9] Otger Steggink and Efrén de la Madre de Dios, *Tiempo y Vida de San Juan de la Cruz* (Madrid: Biblioteca de Autores Cristianos, 1992).

reform was governed by a large number of *conversos* found inside the convents and monasteries. Also, many new Christians gave financial assistance for building new convents and monasteries by supporting the Teresian communities.

This social phenomenon could prove once more that Teresa and perhaps John were well aware of their *converso* backgrounds. Was John one of the many *conversos* who enter the Carmelite Order? I believe that John might have been a *converso* for several reasons: 1) family lineage (John's father and mother were probably Jewish and Muslim *conversos*); 2) circle of *converso* friends (inside and outside the monastic walls); 3) strong Jewish and Muslim presence in places in which he lived (Fontiveros, Medina del Campo, Toledo, Granada, Sevilla, Córdoba, Caravaca de la Cruz, and many others); 4) number of persecutions and personal attacks he had to endure (by his own Carmelite brothers and inquisitors alike); 5) apparent silence, which speaks volumes (notably coming from a learned person like him); 6) forced exile (in la Peñuela before he was almost sent to Mexico); and 7) process of beatification and canonization long overdue (especially if it is compared to the process of other acclaimed saints).

The fact is, nonetheless, that John joined the Teresian reform in 1568 and changed his Calced Carmelite habit for the Discalced, adopting in this new conversion the name of Juan de la Cruz (John of the Cross). The adoption of his new religious name could be viewed as a new rebirth in his life by leaving behind his Calced Carmelite habit and being reborn as a Discalced Carmelite to a new life in Christ. From now on, John and Teresa would work together as the cofounders and coadjutors of the Discalced Carmelite tradition. John would become the spiritual father and founder of the Discalced Carmelite friars, and Teresa the spiritual mother and founder of the Discalced Carmelite nuns.

The Teresian reform left room for manual labor, mental prayer, and the ministry of the sacraments. The Discalced Carmelites spent most of the day in silence. During their time for recreation, they broke the silence by reciting poems, singing songs, playing the flute, and even dancing. They were also allowed to preach and to go on spiritual retreats to caves inside the mountains, like the ancient hermits of Palestine.

The Carmelite Order, from its beginnings, was devoted to a contemplative and austere life. The holy prophet Elijah lived as a hermit on Mount Carmel. Elijah prayed in silence, listening to the still small voice within. Yet, Elijah was a prophetic mystic not only in the sense of witnessing God's Word but also one who announces the deepest troubles of his own society. He did not withdraw from the world for its own sake. Hermits traditionally received visits from friends and spiritual seekers in search of wisdom and practical advice.

By the thirteenth century, the Carmelites observed the strict rules of the Order of St. Albert, striving to imitate the patron and founder of the Carmelite tradition, the prophet Elijah. The first Carmelites adopted the hermit life as a model of desert spirituality within their religious order in the pursuit of solitude and pure contemplation. But this model was never intended to replace a life of prayer in community. The thirteenth century Carmelites erected foundations "not only in desert places but in villages and towns, and thus abandoned the strictly eremitical life."[10]

The Teresian reform did not break with the thirteenth century Carmelite tradition. On August 24, 1562, Teresa founded her first reformed convent, named after St. Joseph, in the inner domains of the city of Ávila where many Jewish *conversos* live, especially those who belong to the middle-class status. Scholars often argue that the Teresian reform was an attempt to return to the primitive rule of St. Albert given to the hermits on Mt. Carmel about 1206-1214. Ironically, Teresa founded the first Discalced Carmelite convent inside the famous medieval walls of Ávila, located at the heart of the inner city. Teresa moved away from her previous religious life as a nun in the Convent of the Incarnation, situated in the outer limits of Ávila, and built her first religious foundation in an urban setting.

---

[10] Fr. Benedict Zimmerman, "The Development of Mysticism in the Carmelite Order," in *The Ascent of Mount Carmel*, ed. and trans. David Lewis (London: Thomas Baker, 1928), 3.

Teresa left her religious sisters practical instructions of how to live the Carmelite reform. Teresa broke with the monastic norms of her first inhabited Convent of the Incarnation by limiting the number of nuns to thirteen. There were more than three hundred nuns living in the Incarnation.

Furthermore, Teresa did not allow wealthy nuns to bring their personal servants, breaking away from her old monastic days in the Incarnation when *beatas* and aristocratic women brought with them their societal habits and prestige. As a result, Teresa avoided future problems and tensions in her new monastic order by getting rid of the master-servant mentality of her feudalist society. Without doubt, Teresa created a more egalitarian society within her religious order. The wealthy nuns did not get a break this time from their religious duties in the Discalced Carmelite Order. Teresa instructed that every nun should obey the prioress and do the assigned works of the day. This is just one of the many social implications of the Teresian reform.

Additionally, Teresa decided that the convent would have no endowment, "news that infuriated the citizens of Ávila,"[11] because they already had enough mendicants to support. Castile was economically in decline. But endowments came with stipulations. Because the wealthy aristocratic families usually provided an income for an endowed religious house, they asked in return to be buried in the community's church and to have the community pray for the salvation of their souls. Teresa, aware of the social environment, wished to be free of debts to benefactors. She survived, thanks to relatively few benefactors like Doña Guiomar, who provided them with the material necessities without demanding favors in return.

Surprisingly, the Discalced Carmelite Order was still searching for approval. Teresa was sent to the Convent of the Incarnation as prioress in 1571, while her religious foundations were paralyzed and suffered delay for several years. In the meantime, Teresa had a clash with her Provincial. Three years later, she was ordered to go to Pastrana where the now

---

[11]Flinders, *Enduring Grace*, 172.

widowed Princess of Eboli had absolute control over the religious nuns. During her stay in Pastrana, Teresa painfully learned that the Princess of Eboli had gotten a copy of her autobiographical manuscript and sent it to a tribunal of the Inquisition in the city of Sevilla. Some viewed her writings with suspicion, because Teresa's illuminations might have raised serious heretical questions. But she was never found unorthodox.

Teresa's reform nevertheless became a reality. The Prior General of the Carmelite Order, John Rossi, encouraged her to open more convents in Castile. From 1566 to 1582, the date of her death, she had founded seventeen Discalced Carmelite convents and four monasteries, from Burgos in the north to Sevilla in the south. As Teresa's relationship with St. John of the Cross grew, so did the number of religious foundations. By this time, people called Teresa "*la* Santa" (the Saint), or "*la Madre Fundadora*" (the Founding Mother).

Teresa indeed fulfilled her dreams of reforming the Carmelite tradition, even though she was a Jewish *converso* woman living in a time when the Church still denied women access to leadership positions. Teresa survived an intolerant climate, especially when ecclesiastical authorities still forbade women to preach and to teach, following St. Paul's alleged prohibition (a controversial biblical passage and one which modern Christian scholars today believe was not written by Paul himself):

> *Let your women keep silence in the churches: for it is not permitted unto them to speak; but they are commanded to be under obedience, as also saith the law. And if they will learn anything, let them ask their husbands at home: for it is a shame for women to speak in the church (1 Cor. 14:34-37).*

Nevertheless, Teresa became the foundress of the Discalced Carmelites, one of the first monastic communities ever founded by a woman. In addition, she had great success as a religious reformer, a spiritual counselor, a mystical writer, a reader of scripture, a practitioner of mental prayer, and a skillful businesswoman and administrator. Having John as her religious co-founder helped the reform reach unthinkable height, especially in a period of time when the kingdom of Castile suffered a great economic crisis.

By joining the Teresian reform in 1567, John found his place in the monastic world. He learned from his travels with Teresa how to build the new religious foundations for nuns and later for friars. John fully embraced the Discalced Carmelite tradition.

The word "discalced" literally means "unshod." But the sixteenth century Spanish Carmelites did not walk barefoot. Instead, they were allowed to use sandals. Why did Teresa adopt for their reform the word "discalced" rather than "calced" (often associated with the Strict Observants of the Carmelite Rule)? Perhaps the Discalced Carmelites knew that the best way to prepare the soul for the coming of the Lord was by detaching oneself from all that is not God. Detachment is a common word used both by Teresa and John in their writings. They used several words to convey this idea: "*desasimiento*," "*anonadamiento*," "*dejamiento*," "*vacío*," "*desnudez*," or "*desapego*."

The first Discalced Carmelites did not reject or withdraw from the world for its own sake. On the contrary, the Carmelites saw God's presence reflected in the world. God's essence is hidden from the visible world, but God's divine attributes are visible since God is the Creator of the universe. The Carmelite's goal is to become closer to God so that the contemplative learns how to see God in all things. By sharing the fruits of contemplation with other human beings, the Carmelite serves God by building the kingdom of God here on earth. Incidentally, the Hebrew word for "Carmel" (רְמֶלֶכ) is translated as God's garden or paradise. Both Teresa and John embodied the ideal of Carmel by planting the seeds of contemplation in their religious order.

On November 28, 1568, John and a senior friar named Antonio de Heredia (later known in religious circles as Antonio de Jesús), founded at Duruelo the first male house following the Teresian ideal. From then on John and Teresa would work together building new Carmelite monasteries and convents and traveling throughout Spain and Portugal.

Among the administrative and religious tasks that John had to fulfill in the earliest stages of his monastic order were the establishment of new Carmelite houses for nuns and friars, and the spiritual direction of novices. The first Discalced Carmelite friary built in Duruelo was a tremendous victory for the Teresian reform. By extending the reform to male houses of the religious order, Teresa has fulfilled her dream by opening Carmelite houses for nuns and friars. No woman ever before Teresa was allowed to become the foundress of a religious order for friars.

John was appointed subprior and novice master of the first Discalced Carmelite friary of Duruelo in 1570. John also held other important administrative positions within the Carmelite Order. In June of the same year, John became master of novices at the Carmelite foundations of Mancera de Abajo and Pastrana. He guided the Carmelite novices in their intellectual and spiritual development. The Teresian reform encouraged and almost required them to combine mental and spiritual exercises with apostolic service. They served in their monastic duties as confessors, preachers, and administrators, and were required to perform manual labor during certain hours of the day. This is further evidence that the Discalced Carmelites embraced the mixed life.

In the spring of 1571, John was transferred to Alcalá de Henares. In April, John was appointed rector of the Carmelite College of Alcalá de Henares. His famous lectures and his spiritual guidance attracted people from all walks of life. He often met with lay university professors for discussions in public and in private. John integrated in his curriculum the study of theology and philosophy so that the students were ready to discern, with the help of a spiritual director or confessor, the mysteries of life.

Teresa knew how important it was for the Carmelite friars to dedicate part of their monastic life to studying their tradition and the Scriptures so that they would meet the spiritual needs of their community. As a result, the Discalced Carmelites gained some independence from the dictates of ecclesiastical authorities who often sent Dominicans or Jesuits to supervise their reform.

At Teresa's request, John left Alcalá to attend to the religious needs of the nuns in Ávila. In 1572, John was appointed the vicar, spiritual director, and confessor at the Convent of the Incarnation. John spent approximately five years working closely with Teresa. He held that office until 1577, when he was kidnapped in Ávila and later arrested in Toledo in that same year. He was held for nine months captive in a Calced Carmelite monastery.

Most commentators believe that the tug of war between Calced and Discalced Carmelites culminated in the incarceration of John in Toledo. He was accused of "rebellion and contumacy" against the Carmelite Order. He had been shut up in a cupboard, six feet by ten, through the bitter cold of the Toledan winter, and the scorching heat of the summer. "Imprisonment, flogging, fasting on bread and water were standards penalties in religious orders of the period," Peter Slattery notes.[12]

In 1578, John escaped from prison after nine months of captivity. It is said that he finally managed to escape from the monastery at night, by tearing his bedding into strips to use as a rope to climb down the steep stone walls. He then made his way through the city to a convent of Reformed nuns, who sheltered him and nursed him back to a semblance of health. He then travelled to Madrid, and from there to El Calvario [where he became the vicar]. He was now no longer in immediate danger, as the attempts to halt the Reform had, at least temporarily, slowed down.[13]

Although political disputes within the Carmelite Order were numerous, I believe there were other hidden motives behind John's persecutions. Why would he be persecuted by both Calced and Discalced Carmelite brothers? It cannot simply be said that John suffered persecution because he was on Teresa's side. I suspect that John's *converso* background played an

---

[12]Slattery, *The Springs of Carmel*, 71.

[13]Caroline McCutcheon, "The Cross of a Friend," *Sufi: A Journal in Sufism* (Spring 1995): 11.

important role, especially in the later persecutions at the hands of his Discalced Carmelite brothers.

It is well known that John wrote some of his poems in prison. He saved them before leaving the prison cell. Some commentators saw John's episode in prison as providential because he had the time to grow intellectually and spiritually in the prison cell, although I do not share that view. It would be very difficult to prove whether John had his first prose commentaries ready prior to or after the tragic episode of Toledo. In addition, John might very well have had some mystical experiences before being kidnapped and put in prison. Therefore, John's dark night should not necessarily be associated with his imprisonment in Toledo.

In 1579, John arrived at Beas of Segura in Andalusia. He stayed with the Carmelite nuns at Beas, recovering from the harsh disciplines and wounds that he received during his imprisonment. In the meantime, John shared his experiences with the nuns, reciting his famous poems to them in the hours of recreation. The scholarly tradition attributed to him, during his stay in Beas, the "Sketch of the Mount," some of the *Sayings of Light and Love*, and some of the commentaries of the *Spiritual Canticle,* and the *Dark Night*. If this is correct, then, those who saw John's imprisonment in Toledo as the quintessential experience of the dark night fail to acknowledge that his commentaries on the dark night were written after his captivity, not in jail.

In the same year, John founded in the university city of Baeza another Carmelite house of studies and become its first rector. Baeza could not compete with Salamanca and Alcalá, but at least attracted a great number of *letrados*, or learned people. John became well acquainted with the professors and the spiritual atmosphere that the town was experiencing at the time. He organized and presided over conferences dealing with spiritual and moral issues. John was not oblivious to the acute problems of his society. He offered the possibility for the whole community to discuss the social and religious problems of his time, sometimes meeting at the Carmelite house of studies or in different private households. It is well documented that his circle of friends included not only religious members of different monastic orders, but also lay people (mostly university professors and people from all walks of life).

Baeza was the location that John of Ávila, the apostle of Andalusia, had chosen for his evangelization. He was a contemporary of St. John of the Cross. It is not a small coincidence that John of Ávila too came from a Jewish *converso* stock. He, like Teresa and John, suffered persecutions. The inquisitors had their eyes on him. Between 1532 and 1533, John of Ávila spent time in prison because of his social critique and his apparent association with certain illuminist sects. Teresa had kept correspondence with the apostle of Andalusia for some time, especially between 1568 and 1569, the date of his death. He greatly influenced the Teresian reform by showing how apostolic action springs from the interior life. Certainly, Teresa's religious order embraced John of Ávila's views on the mixed life.

John had the opportunity to follow John of Ávila's footsteps by exploring the Andalusian region mostly on foot and sometimes on a mule. In fact, the Carmelite saint was introduced to John of Ávila's circle of *converso* friends while he lived in Baeza. The Jewish *converso* population built a strong community around university centers and maintained leadership positions at all social levels. Juan de Ávila was appointed rector of the University of Baeza and patron of the town prior to John's arrival.

Preachers, priests, monks, nuns, and *beatas* (lay women) formed the spiritual geography of Baeza, famous for keeping a great number of *alumbrados*, or illuminist sects, and new Christians. Indeed, it was dangerous for religious people at that time to practice recollection because they could easily be accused of heresy. Both illuminist and Carmelite sects stressed the interior life, but they differed in their methods and understanding on how to live the spiritual life.

By the end of 1581, John had invited Teresa to go with him for the opening of a Carmelite convent at Granada, in Cuesta Gomérez. She rejected the invitation because she felt very ill, and she needed to stay in Ávila as an elected prioress because she was aware of the low morale and bad administration of the nuns at St. Joseph. This was the last time that the two met. In 1582, Teresa left Ávila to found her last convent at Burgos. She was already suffering from what modern medicine calls an internal cancer. She died on October 4 in Alba de Tormes, after her tortuous return journey from Burgos.

In 1582, John arrived in Granada. He made the trip with Ana de Jesús as foundress of the new convent of Carmelite nuns in the city of Granada. John was appointed prior of the Monastery of los Mártires in Granada, next to the palace and gardens of la Alhambra, the last vestige of the Moorish presence in the Iberian Peninsula. From 1582 to 1588, John held the positions of prior of los Mártires and vicar provincial of Andalusia with his residence in Granada. He was also elected second definitor of the Discalced Carmelite Order and first councilor of Doria's *consulta* (or new council).

Granada was a place of inspiration for the mystical theologian and poet. John also designed the new Carmelite foundation for the friars. Three centuries later the religious house was reportedly destroyed by fire, as some Carmelite commentators suggested. However, Miguel F. de Haro Iglesias, ex-prior of the Discalced Carmelite monastery in Granada and director of the Spanish journal, *San Juan de la Cruz*, told me, in one of my last trips to Spain, that he is convinced the Carmelite foundation was simply demolished after the friars were forced to leave the convent. Reports tell us that the religious edifice had the most beautiful cloister of the Carmelite Order.

Additionally, John has been recognized for having built an aqueduct with his own hands and the help of his brother Francisco. The aqueduct not only brought water from the site of la Alhambra but also created a spiritual atmosphere used for contemplation. The artistic elements built upon the aqueduct and the proximity to the Alhambra Palace and Gardens offer the friars and guests a place to renew their spirit. By irrigating the desert hills of los Mártires, a place known for Muslim soldiers having kept Christian captives underneath the earth, John fulfilled the Carmelite ideal of envisioning a paradise or spiritual garden on earth. Today the area is fertile and full of vegetation. The aqueduct is still well preserved. As E. Allison Peers states:

> *He [John] also took part in the building which was going on when he arrived, mixing the sand and lime and making bricks like any labourer ... A second house had already been built and a reservoir constructed for the supply of necessary water. The additions made in John's time were some further buildings, an aqueduct and a cloister.*[14]

Interestingly, the Major of the Alhambra Palace and Generalife yielded part of its water right to the Carmelites, which caused them several lawsuits, after the President of the Real Chancillería (formerly, a Spanish High Court of Justice) denounced them for having used tons of water. Philip II solved the problem, by conceding license and money to the Carmelite foundation, and having John as the prior. This proves once again the link between politics, religion, and spirituality in John's active ministry.

Some say that John also planted an old Mexican cedar next to the aqueduct. The Carmelite friars who served as missionaries in Mexico brought the cedar tree (actually a cypress) to the Iberian Peninsula. The tree could link John to the New World. In the words of biological researchers, Manuel Casares and José Tito: "La presencia del árbol había sido expuesta por San Juan del Cruz, que lo recogía en sus textos como representación de la altura y perfección del amor o como creador del ambiente propicio para la unión mística."[15]

According to the researchers, the SanJuanist tree is the oldest species in Europe. It was brought up from Mexico via Portugal. The botanists named it "*Cupressus lusitánica.*" Spanish biologists from the University of Granada

---

[14]Peers, E. Allison. *Spirit of Flame: A Study of St. John of the Cross*. (New York: Morehouse-Gorham, 1945) 77.

[15]Juan Enrique Gómez, "El árbol más viejo: San Juan de la Cruz escribía junto a él en el convento," *Ideal* 9 (October 1997): 12. Gómez writes: "The presence of the tree had been described by St. John of the Cross in his writings as a representation of the height and perfection of love, or as the creator of an adequate environment for the mystical union" [my own translation].

are raising awareness about the uniqueness and importance of the tree in question, because it is one of the oldest in Europe and forms an integral part of the SanJuanist legacy in the city of Granada.

During his fruitful years in Granada, John finished writing his major prose commentaries on his four mystical poems: the *Ascent of Mount Carmel*; the *Dark Night*; the *Spiritual Canticle*; and the *Living Flame of Love*. In all his works, John presented themes familiar in the Christian mystical tradition: union between the lover and the beloved (*unio mystica*); and a creative synthesis between faith and reason, between poetry and prose (biblical commentaries), between the mystic and the theologian, between the apophatic and cataphatic, between experience (vision) and articulation of that mystical experience (voice), between the dark and the light (the luminous darkness), between *la nada* (no-thing) *y el todo* (the all).

At the request of Ana de Peñalosa and Ana de Jesús, John wrote and explained in his theological commentaries the rich symbols of his poems by interpreting for his readers the nature and stages of the mystical experience. He often recited his poems aloud to the nuns and the lay people who were his guests or visitors. Teresa used to tell her nuns and friars to rejoice in their time of recreation. By singing, dancing, or reciting poems the Carmelites built a spirituality of the ordinary where the senses are sublimated.

The sixteenth century Carmelites lived a simple life dedicated to God. For the Carmelites, the apparently ordinary activities in life (such as washing dishes and reciting poems) were elevated to the state of the extraordinary as they undertook such daily tasks as manual labor, intellectual exercises, and devotional practices. Thus, the spiritual seeker finds comfort and joy in the Spanish Carmelite tradition because the monastic tradition addresses the needs of the whole person, including body, mind, and soul.

During the demolition of the old minaret tower (known as the Turpian tower) in the cathedral of Granada in 1588, workers found religious relics and manuscripts probably written by Moorish *conversos* Alonso del Castillo or Miguel de Luna. Also, the twenty-two *"libros plúmbeos"* discovered in the Sacro Monte (located in the hills of Valparaíso) prove the legacy of the last *moriscos* living in the kingdom of Granada after the expulsion of the Moors in 1492. These controversial books apparently written by *moriscos* included cabalistic inscriptions and crypto-Muslim codes written in Latin.

Archbishop Don Juan Méndez de Salvatierra named a committee (or *Junta Magna*) of ecclesiastical authorities and theologians to study the authenticity of the manuscripts. John of the Cross was included in the list as one of the leading theologians who participated in this study. They concluded that the relics and the manuscripts found in the cathedral were authentic. However, in May 1588, with the death of the archbishop, the process stopped. In 1682, Pope Inocence XI condemned the texts as apocryphal.

John spent a great number of years in Granada. He was reelected three times as a prior and then nominated as vicar provincial or superior of Andalusia at a chapter in Lisbon in 1585. This last position obliged him to travel and build more foundations. It is estimated that he traveled about 27, 000 kilometers (about 16,777 miles) during his lifetime.[16]

These events demonstrate the link between the active life and the contemplative life in John's ministry. In reality, John was a very successful prior, administrator, and mystic. As a prior and administrator, John had to solve problems in the Carmelite community on a daily basis. Proof of his achievements is the fact that he was elected prior of Granada many times, and he held other important leadership roles within the Discalced Carmelite Order.

In 1588, John was sent to Segovia to become the prior of the Carmelite Monastery of Segovia. He was also elected third councilor to the vicar general of the Discalced Carmelite Order, Father Nicolás Doria. John did not get along well with Doria, especially after the vicar general ordered a reprisal against Ana de Jesús, one of Teresa's and John's loyal friends. In spite of Doria, Ana became the prioress of Beas and Granada. She later founded convents in Belgium and France. John wrote the *Spiritual*

---

[16] Ibid.

Canticle's commentaries at her request. These writings were first published in France with the consent of Ana de Jesús in 1622.

Doria proposed to centralize the Carmelite government of the religious order by gaining control over the jurisdiction of convents and monasteries. Of course, the nuns were against these measures and John supported the nuns' cause. Then Doria removed him from his administrative duties and sent him to the desert of la Peñuela to a hermitage. John was sent there as punishment after having a personal confrontation with Doria's policies.

In 1591, John suffered new attacks. This time Doria wanted to remove him from the Iberian Peninsula by sending him to Mexico as a missionary. John, being a person of discernment, was sensitive to the injustices and corruption of his time. Like his predecessor, the famous theologian and bishop of Chiapas, Bartolomé de las Casas, who fought for the rights of the Indians against the Castilian settlers, John struggled within his Discalced Carmelite Order to champion the rights of the nuns and monks to govern themselves according to local forms of government. As the Carmelite Peter Slattery rightly observes: "Certainly, toward the end of his [John's] life those with power did not want him close to them."[17]

John became very ill. He suffered from fevers and gangrenous sores on his foot. He moved from the convent of la Peñuela (today located in la Carolina) to Úbeda, where he received poor treatment from the prior, Friar Francisco Crisóstomo, who even denied him medical attention. John died on December 14, 1591.

On January 22, 1675, Clement X beatified John of the Cross, a beatification that took longer than was expected, for St. Ignatius of Loyola and St. Teresa of Ávila (1614) were beatified right after their deaths. In 1726, Benedict XIII canonized him. On August 24, 1926, St. John of the Cross "was solemnly declared a Doctor of the Universal Church"[18] by Pope Pius XI. In

---

[17]Slattery, *The Springs of Carmel*, 74.

[18]Father Gabriel of St. Mary Magdalen, *St. John of the Cross: Doctor of Divine Love and Contemplation* (Westminster, Maryland: The Newman Press, 1954), xi. Pope Pio XI proclaimed St. John of the Cross "*Doctor Ecclesiae*" in his Apostolic Letter *Die Vicesima*. For many SanJuanist

1970, Teresa was the first woman to be granted this title by Pope Paul VI. In 1952, the Spanish Ministry of National Education named St. John of the Cross the patron of Spanish poets.

In life, John was a contemplative in search of solitude; yet he was well known for his extraordinary social skills, for his respect shown to everyone, including his enemies. John was an ordinary man who worked hard and never complained about it, because he did it for the love of God and for the love of neighbor. While on his death bed, John listened to the verses from the *Song of Songs*, his favorite mystical text. His witnesses saw John's compassionate heart in action when, on the eve of his death, he forgave the prior of Úbeda for his mistreatment.

As a result of his merciful actions, John demonstrated to his fellow Carmelites that his spirit was full of generosity and kindness, even when he suffered in his own flesh the physical afflictions and personal attacks initiated by some of his religious brothers and superiors. John taught that the virtue of compassion is not an abstract thought, but ought to be manifested through deeds. Without a full understanding of John's life events, his thoughts are meaningless because his works contain the language and learned experiences of his lifetime.

Posthumously, John's manuscripts were known only to a small circle of readers and friends of the Carmelite saint. In 1618, John's works were published in Alcalá de Henares under the editorial revisions of Diego de Jesús Salablanca. However, the *Spiritual Canticle* was deliberately left out. It was reprinted in Barcelona in 1619. The text was denounced to the Inquisition. Friar Luis de León's second cousin, Basilio Ponce de León, who was himself an Augustinian friar and professor of theology at Salamanca, successfully defended John's writings against any accusations of heresy. This event demonstrates the possibility that John and Luis knew each other. Friar Luis was a professor of theology at Salamanca while John was a student. Besides that, Friar Luis was the main editor of Teresa's completed

---

specialists the year 1926 marks the turning point of future critical studies once John has become the *"Doctor Misticus"* of the Catholic Church.

works. Along with this evidence, twentieth-century researchers have demonstrated that both Teresa and Luis were descendants of Jewish *converso* (convert) families.

Before John's texts were published and made available to the public, they suffered serious scrutiny by censors, inquisitors, and ecclesiastical authorities. Some *letrados* (scholars) denounced John's writings for containing some of the heresies of illuminism and of quietism detected in different parts of the kingdoms of Castile and Aragon. However, John's writings were never condemned as being heretical by the Catholic Church. There is indeed a very fine line between John's mystical orthodox teachings and the heresies of *alumbrados* (the illuminists) and that of *dejados* (the quietists).

The first edition of the *Spiritual Canticle* was published in French in Paris in 1622. However, the first Spanish edition was published in Brussels in 1627 with the help of Ana de Jesús. Spain would have to wait until 1630 for someone to publish the first edition of the complete works in Spanish. This edition was prepared by Jerónimo de San José in Madrid and was also denounced to the Inquisition.

The first English translation of St. John of the Cross's completed works appeared in England in 1864. David Lewis's two volume edition, *The Completed Works of St. John of the Cross* (London: Thomas Baker, 1864), included a preface by Cardinal Wiseman. Nonetheless the two most important English translations in the twentieth century are the editions of E. Allison Peers, and of Kieran Kavanaugh and Otilio Rodríguez. In *The Completed Works of St. John of the Cross, Doctor of the Church* (London: Burns Oates & Washbourne, 1934), Peers has adopted Father Silverio's Spanish critical edition. Kavanaugh and Rodríguez's *The Collected Works of St. John of the Cross* (Washington, DC: ICS Publications, 1973), is the most accurate and most often quoted English translation in our times.

In this study, I am using Kavanaugh and Rodríguez's collected edition because their translation more accurately reflects the new developments in the modern English language. However, Peers' translation would be more appealing to those readers who are looking for an old-fashioned version of John's writings. In this regard, Peers did a phenomenal job capturing the poetic tone of John's writings in the language of Shakespeare.

In a few instances where translators fail to capture the meaning behind the SanJuanist expressions, I chose to translate those selected poems that were relevant for this study. In most cases, English translations fail to address the meaning of John's poetry either by engendering the original poetic version in Spanish or by overlooking important aspects of John's mystical poems. My method of translation incorporates both literal and allegorical renditions. I also translated most of the Spanish texts that are not available in English or cannot easily be found in bookstores or libraries.

John's writings are mainly composed of his four major commentary treatises on his mystical poems (the *Ascent of Mount Carmel*, the *Dark Night*, the *Spiritual Canticle*, and the *Living Flame of Love*), his less famous poems (ten "romances" or ballads, five poetical "glosses," and two other poems), his shorter prose works (the *Sayings of Light and Love,* the *Precautions, Counsels to a Religious, Censure and Opinion*), and the few letters that survive many years of correspondence (only thirty-three letters). As Leonard Doohan indicates:

> *In the year before he died, some of John's writings were destroyed by nuns concerned about the nasty insinuations of Diego Evangelista. None of the original manuscripts of John's major works remains; the longest autograph is the twelve pages of the Sayings of Light and Love. We also have some of his original letters, and an early copy of the Canticle in another hand, with what may be John's handwritten corrections added, but nothing else. Fortunately, his works have come to us through numerous copies, which are more or less faithful. This raises the need for critical scholarship to determine the most accurate original reading.*[19]

---

[19]Leonard Doohan, *The Contemporary Challenge of John of the Cross: An Introduction to His Life and Teaching* (Washington, District of Columbia: ICS Publications, 1995), 24.

The missing documents, such as baptismal certificates and letters, and the nature of the incomplete writings of St. John of the Cross, have not only left us with a sense of loss but also with the necessity to reconstruct John's world, assuming that most of his collected writings and personal testimonies bear witness to his life and thoughts.

It is, therefore, not difficult to understand now why it took so many decades, even centuries, before John was beatified, canonized, and given the honorific title of Mystical Doctor of the Catholic Church. Ironically, John's texts became the norm for testing the authenticity of what could be regarded as the model of sainthood and nowadays called by Pope Francis the model of holiness. Priests, monks, and theologians, especially in seminaries, still spend many hours studying John's writings. They see him as an authority in matters of faith. In an apostolic letter dated December 14, 1990, Pope John Paul II, who wrote his doctoral dissertation on St. John of the Cross, dedicates a whole document to the Carmelite saint calling him a "master in the faith" and a "witness of the living God."

Today, people from all walks of life (particularly religious figures, poets, scientists, artists, philosophers, theologians, atheists, and so forth) have demonstrated a special interest in studying John's life and writings. The studies on St. John of the Cross have increased dramatically in the twentieth century. Researchers from an array of fields of knowledge have discovered new data on the historical background and the life events of the Carmelite saint, on the authenticity of his writings, and on the originality of his thoughts. This work reconsiders the life and the thoughts of St. John of the Cross in light of these scholarly studies.

Again, this study will provide an inquiry into the often-ignored prophetic element in the works of the Carmelite saint. That inquiry will begin in the following chapter, which is perhaps the most valuable chapter in this book. It will introduce the mystical path of action in St. John of the Cross.

3

THE MYSTICAL PATH OF ACTION

"Mi alma se ha empleado,
y todo mi caudal en su servicio."
(poem from *the Spiritual Canticle*)

"My soul and all my wealth
are employed in [God's] service."
(My own translation)

Metaphorically speaking, the "body" is that part of the human person that performs "the actual activity of man on earth."[1] The metaphor of the "body" is connected with the Hindu philosophy of *karma yoga*, since this corporeal function of the human self symbolizes action. For Christians, it means the way of apostolic service. Robert Neville calls it the path of the "soldier." For instance, it is well known in the history of Christianity that St. Ignatius of Loyola called himself a soldier of Christ. Ignatius had been. in real life, a soldier, but after being wounded in battle and having been born again in Christ, he offered his life to the service of God. For Panikkar, the symbol that best represents the path of action is the element of earth. In the SanJuanist concordance index the word "earth" is cited 130 times.[2]

---

[1] Raimundo Panikkar, *Worship and Secular Man* (Maryknoll, New York: Orbis Books, 1973), 87.

[2] Juan Luis Astigarraga, Agustí Borrell, and F. Javier Martín de Lucas, eds. *Concordancias de los escritos de San Juan de la Cruz* (Roma: Teresianum, 1990), 1797-1799.

The mystical path of action has been overlooked by both SanJuanist scholars and by readers. John uses the Spanish word "*obras*" in two ways: Sometimes it could mean "works" in the religious sense of the word (apostolic works). But it could also mean acquired contemplation, understood as a spiritual discipline that prepares the soul to receive God. John's notion of "work" is understood in the context of his teachings on spiritual attachment. For instance, John says:

> *God is more pleased by one work, however small, done secretly, without desire that it be known, than a thousand done with the desire that people know of them. Those who work for God with purest love not only care nothing about whether others see their works, but do not even seek that God himself know of them. Such persons would not cease to render God the same services, with the same joy and purity of love, even if God were never to know of these.*[3]

The ascetico-mystical teachings of St. John of the Cross underline the Christic kenotic message of detachment from one's own fruits. John's mystical theology of detachment teaches us how to work for the love of God without expecting heavenly or societal rewards. The human soul that loves God must not desire any other reward for his or her services than the unconditional love of God. In fact, John writes: "The pure and whole work done for God in a pure heart merits a whole kingdom for its owner."[4] Additionally, John states that some seek recognition or fame without undertaking their works for the love of God. "It can be said that in these works some adore themselves more than God."[5] In short, John's theology of detachment can be summarized in the following words written by the Carmelite saint in the *Precautions*:

> *The second precaution is that you should never give up your works because of a want of satisfaction and delight in them, if they are fitting*

---

[3] John of the Cross, *The Collected Works*, 86-87; *Sayings of Light and Love* 20.

[4] Ibid., 87; *Sayings of Light and Love* 21.

[5] Ibid., 319; *Ascent of Mount Carmel* 3.28.5.

for the service of God. Neither should you carry out these works merely because of the satisfaction or delight they accord you, but you should do them just as you would the disagreeable ones. Otherwise it will be impossible for you to gain constancy and conquer your weakness.[6]

The SanJuanist notion of martyrdom is also tied to John's notion of the love of God and his understanding of the mystery of the cross. The word "martyr" means witness. And many Christians think of John as a martyr of love, as a witness to God's presence in the world. But nonetheless, John sought God through works. Like Teresa, John knew that faith without works is futile and sterile. Their spiritual resistance to those who abuse the authority invested in them shows the level of commitment and personal sacrifice of the two cofounders of the Discalced Carmelite Order.

As we have seen, both Teresa and John suffered persecution in their lifetime. In 1576, at the age of sixty-two, Teresa was interrogated by the inquisitors in Sevilla after a novice from the Carmelite foundation of that city, María del Corro, denounced her of being a quietist (or "*dejada*") or an illuminist (or "*alumbrada*"). But the Inquisition never found Teresa guilty of any heresy. Hence, it would be erroneous to call Teresa a quietist or an illuminist, because her method of recollection is closer to the religious practice of *recogidos*; that is to say, she is one of those who are drawn to live a deeper interior life within the parameters of the Roman Catholic Church, including such religious activities as attending Mass on a daily basis, receiving the eucharist, or confessing with a priest.

Quietists, in contrast, advocated "direct, ecstatic contact with God for lay people as well as professional religious"[7] through contemplative prayer, and their religious practice focused on self-abandonment of all external devotion in favor of interior passivity and inspiration in similar fashion to Lutheran spirituality. Those practices applied with particular intensity to women called *beatas,* who most often came from *converso* families.

---

[6] Ibid., 724; *Precautions* 16.

[7] Flinders, *Enduring Grace,* 160.

In 1559, the Index of Forbidden Books banned several Spanish works on mental prayer. Among these books are those read by Teresa and most certainly by John, namely Francisco de Osuna's *The Third Spiritual Alphabet* and some commentaries by Friar Luis de Granada. Indeed, the Inquisitors saw mental prayer "as a screen for Protestant pietism and other forms of heterodox belief, and as a means of avoiding the control of the Church hierarchy."[8] This is why the *letrados*, usually Dominicans and Jesuits, were deeply suspicious of mental prayer – believing, rather, that "theological studies provided the only knowledge one could have of God in this life."[9]

In addition to John's imprisonment in Toledo, the Carmelite saint suffered false accusations and personal attacks under the rubric of immoral conduct. Some of his young friars accused him of having kissed one of the nuns in Málaga, Catalina de Jesús. In Granada, a woman claimed that John left her pregnant. Still today people in Granada talk about that incident. Nevertheless, John was never found guilty of any of those accusations.

The nuns of Málaga defended him and saw the malice of those who accused him, namely Ambrosio Mariano and Diego Evangelista. The nuns knew that Catalina was coerced. She later confessed that her accusations against John were false. She was forced to sign a deposition without having read it.[10]

The other case in Granada was solved by John himself, by asking those who accused him for the age of the baby. They replied: one year. And John told them that he had just moved to live in Granada. It was impossible for him to have had an affair with a woman in Granada before he had even arrived there.[11]

---

[8]Ibid., 175-176.

[9]Ibid., 175.

[10]See Silverio de Santa Teresa, *Historia del Carmen Descalzo en España, Portugal y América* (Burgos: El Monte Carmelo, 1936), 639-641.

[11]Ibid., 233.

John's enemies were planning to expel him from the Carmelite Order by any means necessary, especially following Doria's orders. Then, after failing to charge John with false accusations, they proposed sending him to Mexico, but he died before that decision was made.

John, like Teresa, suffered for God and for humanity in order to bring the kingdom of God here on earth, so all his actions were imbedded in love. John understood that the only way to serve God perfectly was to love God unconditionally, without reservations or expectations. Love was his answer. And as he says in the *Spiritual Canticle*, his "sole occupation is to love." John interprets this part of the poem in the following commentary:

> *This is like saying that now all this work is directed to the practice of love of God, that is: All the ability of my soul and body (memory, intellect, and will, interior and exterior senses, appetites of the sensory and spiritual parts) move in love and because of love. Everything I do I do with love, and everything I suffer I suffer with the delight of love.*[12]

As it has been suggested before, the Spanish word for "works" can be used in two ways, depending on the context. Besides apostolic service, John uses it in the context of acquired contemplation, that is, the human effort required to reach out to the divine. Mystical theologians distinguish acquired from infused contemplation by saying that the latter is only achieved by God's grace and the former is a way of preparing the soul to receive God solely by human effort.

Let me examine now one of the most famous passages using "works" following the latter explanation. John writes:

> *It should be noted that until the soul reaches this state of union of love, she should practice love in both the active and contemplative life. Yet once she arrives she should not become involved in other works and exterior exercises that might be of the slightest hindrance to the attentiveness of love toward God, even though the work be of great service to God. For a little of this pure love is more precious to God and*

---

[12] John of the Cross, *The Collected Works*, 586; *Spiritual Canticle* 28.8.

> the soul and more beneficial to the Church, even though it seems one is doing nothing, than all these other works put together.[13]

Again, some scholars have interpreted this passage as if John were a quietist who rejected all human activities, including works of charity, in order to reach union with God. As it has been mentioned earlier in his life events, John clearly integrated a contemplative and prayerful life with a very active apostolic ministry. Although he lived a very active life within the parameters of his religious order, John the monk spent a great part of the day praying, meditating, and celebrating Vespers and other liturgical services. Nevertheless, John's prayerful life was not disconnected from his active life. He surely might have prayed and meditated while traveling, lecturing, preaching, confessing, or building new Carmelite houses.

For Catholics, salvation is not attained by faith alone but also by works. Charity and love are at the heart of Christianity. Without them, the Catholic practitioner cannot attain the highest degree of union with God in this life. And, of course, John was well rooted in the Catholic faith, particularly in the spirituality of his time (mainly, in the Carmelite [Teresian] tradition and in the Ignatian ideal of a contemplative in action).

To conclude that John was a quietist would be a mistake because the Carmelite saint is not denying the importance of apostolic works, or ascetic practices. Rather, John is referring to the total abandonment in God, which is part of the night of passivity or the spirit (or most commonly known in mystical theology as infused contemplation). In this intimate state of union with God one must renounce to all worldly activities so that one can receive God more fully, without distractions. As John clearly states: "since the soul and God are now united in this state of spiritual marriage that we are discussing, the soul performs no work without God."[14]

The works that John is referring to in the last passage are not of apostolic service but rather of mortification and other exterior, ascetic practices.

---

[13] Ibid., 587; *Spiritual Canticle* 29.2.

[14] Ibid., 616; *Spiritual Canticle* 37.6.

Subsequently we should not confuse John's definition of apostolic action with his notion of works as acquired contemplation. What John is trying to explain in those previous passages is that even though Catholics leave room for apostolic work as a way to salvation, works alone do not save one's soul. In other words, John the contemplative is stressing that one blessing or divine touch from the love of God is more beneficial than thousands of ascetic practices.

However, in order to receive God at the deepest center of the soul, one must prepare oneself to a certain degree by performing acts of virtue and devoting oneself to God through fasting, mortification, and other exterior or interior exercises. As a matter of fact, John performed great virtuous acts and practiced many ascetic exercises in his lifetime: taking care of the ill, resisting Doria's efforts to have absolute control over the nuns, sharing the fruits of his contemplative life with lay and religious people, fasting and meditating, are just a few instances.

John not only reveals the prominent role that action plays in the contemplative life but he also acknowledges its shortcoming, particularly the danger of activism. John writes:

> *Let those, then, who are singularly active, who think they can win the world with their preaching and exterior works, observe here that they would profit the Church and please God much more, not to mention the good example they would give, were they to spend at least half of this time with God in prayer, even though they might not have reached a prayer as sublime as this. They would then certainly accomplish more, and with less labor, by one work that they otherwise would by a thousand. For through their prayer they would merit this result, and themselves be spiritually strengthened. Without prayer they would do a great deal of hammering but accomplish little, and sometimes nothing, and even at times cause harm. God forbid that the salt should begin to lose its savor [Mt. 5:13]. However much they may appear to achieve*

> *externally, they will in substance be accomplishing nothing; it is beyond doubt that good works can be performed only by the power of God.*[15]

This passage is perhaps one of the most misunderstood writings of St. John of the Cross. John is not rejecting the active life by favoring the contemplative life. A careful reading suggests that the Carmelite saint as a spiritual director informed the religious seeker of the possible dangers of falling prey to worldly activities (that is, preaching and exterior works) without spending some time with God in prayer. John concludes that "good works can be performed only by the power of God." Thus, God is the agent and power behind every single human act. Yet John does not condemn apostolic service or the active life in itself because every single work dedicated to the glory of God is a labor of love, especially when the religious person offers the fruit of his or her actions to God alone as an act of devotion.

The Carmelite saint was well aware that preachers and missionaries who represent the active life in Christian religious terms criticize monks and nuns (so-called contemplatives) because they give themselves entirely to God without undertaking some of the hardships of ordinary life. He says: "They think these persons are excessive in their conduct, estrangement, and withdrawal, and assert that they are useless in important matters and lost to what the world esteems."[16]

Apostolic service like preaching or undertaking missionary activities could be fruitless without being grounded in faith, hope, and love. The mere task of performing external acts of devotion does not guarantee a positive result if God is not taking the initiative. Without grace all acts are condemned to failure. Works without God's intervention are vain, ineffective, or sterile. Commenting on one of his poems, John declares:

> The flower of these works and virtues is the grace and power they possess from the love of God. Without love these works will not only fail to flower

---

[15] Ibid., 588; *Spiritual Canticle* 29.3.

[16] Ibid; *Spiritual Canticle* 29.5.

but will all wither and become valueless in God's sight, even though they may be perfect from a human standpoint. Yet because God bestows his grace and love, they are works that have blossomed in his love.[17]

Also, faith without human effort can be misleading and futile simply because God requires from the spiritual seeker total collaboration and a certain degree of personal response and serious commitment. John, following a long Christian mystical tradition greatly influenced by the *Song of Songs*, believed that the gift of grace "is not received without the ability and help of the soul receiving it ... But she [the bride] does not state that he alone or she alone runs, but that we shall both run, which means that God and the soul work together."[18]

John's theology of love explains the mutual relationship that exists between God and the human soul by using the analogy of the exchange of love of the bride for the bridegroom in the *Song of Songs*. Based on this mutual love, human works are elevated to a divine status when God pours the gift of grace in the human soul by participation, by sharing the power of love with everything created. The whole universe becomes a "sea of love." John puts it this way:

> *He [God] loves all things for himself; thus, love becomes the purpose for which he loves. He therefore does not love things because of what they are in themselves. With God, to love the soul is to put her somehow in himself and make her his equal. Thus, he loves the soul within himself, with himself, that is, with the very love by which he loves himself. This is why the soul merits the love of God in all her works insofar as she does them in God. Placed in this height, this grace, she merits God himself in every work.*[19]

The habitual practice of love in ordinary life benefits not only the human soul but also everyone. God infuses this loving knowledge to spiritual

---

[17] Ibid., 594; *Spiritual Canticle* 30.8.

[18] Ibid., 593; *Spiritual Canticle* 30.6.

[19] Ibid., 600; *Spiritual Canticle* 32.6.

seekers who are awaiting the coming of the Lord. The human soul is transformed in a divine manner by encountering God at the deepest center of the soul. As a result of that mystical encounter, the blessed soul responds to that act of love by sharing the "good news" with their fellow creatures and the world at large. Consequently, the prophetic mystics are seen by many as the messengers or friends of God. As Elizabeth A. Johnson describes in reference to *sophia*, or divine wisdom:

> *Although she is but one, she can do all things, and while remaining in herself, she renews all things; in every generation she passes into holy souls and makes them friends of God, and prophets.* [Wisdom 7:27]

This text, when applied to the communion of saints, succeeds in structuring those who respond to grace into a circle of companions by the power of Spirit-Sophia. It became the guiding intuition of my exploration.[20]

For Johnson, a saint is not someone who completely ignores the world, but rather one whose religious vision leads to personal and social transformation by changing the perceptions of those who are seeking spiritual guidance. Similarly, in a prayerful passage John writes:

> *That is: Let us rejoice in the communication of the sweetness of love, not only in that sweetness we already possess in our habitual union but in that which overflows into the effective and actual practice of love, either interiorly with the will in the affective act or exteriorly in works directed to the service of the Beloved. As we mentioned, when love takes root it has this characteristic: It makes one always desire to taste the joys and sweetnesses of love in the inward and outward exercise of love. All this the lover does in order to resemble the Beloved more.*[21]

John's distinction between interior and exterior practices of love explains the Carmelite saint's theology of love by bringing asceticism and the mysticism of action together. Hence the perfect balance between action and

---

[20] Elizabeth A. Johnson, *Friends of God and Prophets: A Feminist Theological Reading of the Communion of Saints* (New York: Continuum, 1999), 2.

[21] John of the Cross, *The Collected Works*, 611; *Spiritual Canticle* 36.4.

contemplation, Martha and Mary, apostolic service and faith, could be accomplished if spiritual seekers let God perform the works through them. As John puts it, "it is beyond doubt that good works can be performed only by the power of God."[22] And yet, John the mystic becomes a sort of prophet through both of this gift bestowed on him by God, and his own courage in standing firm in his radical response to the divine message. Thus, John established a reputation himself of being a loyal friend to his Carmelite brothers and sisters, even when they arrested him, imprisoned him, and attacked him personally following Doria's orders.

John, however, summarizes his mystical theology by stressing God's will rather than our will, following the Pauline message of the recapitulation of all things in Christ. John had Jesus Christ as the perfect exemplar of total abandonment in God while he was crucified on the cross. Following the Christian ideal of *imitatio Christi*, John had the desire to imitate Christ out of love. Jesus Christ, who died on the cross for the sins of the world, shows the way.

John as a Christian worshipped and praised God by behaving like Jesus Christ as the role exemplar that he became for all his followers. In the monastic tradition, every single action is consecrated for the honor and glory of God. John repeatedly said that only those who perform works for the love of God will find the kingdom of heaven at hand and within ("Emmanuel"). But even the thought of doing it because one wants to enter into heaven is detrimental to the aspirations of the human soul to become God by participation. As a matter of fact, John writes: "Eat not in forbidden pastures (those of this life), because blessed are they who hunger and thirst for justice, for they will be satisfied [Mt.5:6]. What God seeks, he being himself God by nature, is to make us gods through participation, just as fire converts all things into fire."[23]

---

[22]Ibid., 588; *Spiritual Canticle* 29.3.

[23] Ibid., 93; *Sayings of Light and Love* 107 (in other works is Saying 106).

The golden rule in Christianity is to love God and to love our neighbor. Or as the Bible says: "You shall love your neighbor as yourself" (Leviticus 19:18). In John's words: "Those who do not love their neighbor abhor God."[24] These expressions only made sense when they are read in reference to John's theology of love because they are rooted in the words of the Bible. The Gospel of John says: "Whoever does not love does not know God, for God is love" (1 John 4:8).

The Carmelite saint did not withdraw completely from the world with the intent of escaping from his social or religious environment. Rather, John thought that we can reach the highest degree of perfection by loving God and our neighbors, by executing works for Christ not for ourselves, by performing works in praise of the almighty God.

The rigid asceticism represented by John's doctrinaires stresses the idea of annihilation of all the senses, interior and exterior, by means of killing all desires (even the healthy ones), so the penitent could subdue and mortify all the senses. For instance, Gerald Brenan states that St. John of the Cross "led a life of the most extreme asceticism, starving his body and spending his nights in prayer and contemplation, often by a stream, or under an olive tree, or in a cave looking out on the landscape."[25] However, John's ascetic doctrine is defined within the parameters of a long established biblical and monastic traditions. It might be difficult to reconcile that "masochistic" interpretation of the *via dolorosa*, which accepts suffering as the only way to God, with the incarnational, sacramental teachings of the religion of Jesus in the Gospels and in the Teresian Carmelite reform.

It is difficult to know the reasons behind John's decision to enter the Carmelite Order. But one thing is certain: John the ascetico-mystic has historically taken the place of John as the religious reformer and prophet who was deeply involved in the world. In other words, John's active life is

---

[24] Ibid., 97; *Saying of Light and Love* 167 (in other works is Saying 176).

[25] Gerald Brenan, *The Literature of the Spanish People: From Roman Times to the Present* (New York: Meridian Books, 1967), 160.

overshadowed by his contemplative life. According to Thomas P. McDonnell:

> *Perhaps the chief contradiction about this only fairly bright Doctor of the Church ... is that John of the Cross was a contemplative who was also an activist when the occasion demanded extreme measures. Even in this, however, he was an activist against his own best will and preferences. As between these ancient modalities of our both human and spiritual natures, he by far preferred peace and quiet and contemplation.*[26]

John has been portrayed as a monk who sought to live in complete solitude and in silence by escaping from the world in which he lived. Most hagiographers depicted John praying all day by either sitting in his monastic cell or spending long hours inside mountain caves, following the ascetic-hermit model of Elijah in his ascent to heaven. As Pedro Casaldáliga notes: "The earlier Christian tradition instructed us in a model of prayer that only went up, without coming down. This is graphically suggested in John of the Cross's title, the *Ascent of Mount* Carmel."[27]

To further illustrate this problem, the father of liberation theology in Latin America, Gustavo Gutiérrez, raised serious questions about different readings of John's works. Here is a text that summarizes Gustavo's views on John:

> *But what can there be of interest to us in the saint of the Ascent of Mount Carmel, of the nights and purifications, of betrothals with God, that seem so remote from daily life? What interest can we find in the mystic for whom issues such as social justice seem strange, who never discussed or quoted Luke 4:16 or Matthew 25:31, texts so important in the lives of Christians in Latin America and in our reflection? What can there be of interest to us in this great and admirable Christian who nevertheless seems so remote from our concerns?*[28]

---

[26] Thomas P. McDonnell, *Saints for All Seasons*, ed. John J. Delaney (Garden City, New York: Image Books, 1978), 154-155.

[27] Casaldáliga and Vigil, *Political Holiness*, 103.

[28] Ibid., 209.

Gutiérrez partially responded to those questions by recalling John's "experience of family poverty, and the persecution he suffered for his reforming zeal."[29] To say that John did not care about the world is to ignore his life experiences, to erase from our collective memory the testimonies left by those who knew him, and to be unacquainted with his writings. Thus, the apparent contradictions created in John's name between God vs. the world, God vs. creatures, are not historically sound since they exclude from the Christian mission the duty to love our neighbor and to love the world as a reflection of the *imago dei*.

Katherine Marie Dyckman and L. Patrick Carroll both argue that

> [o]ften the spirituality of our past, so easily caricatured in á Kempis, reflected this neo-Platonic disdain for the body and the negative elements of asceticism: the limiting of pleasure, the crushing of pride and lust, the killing of self-love, the mortification of the senses. But our Redeemer prayed that "joy mabe be in you, and your joy may be complete" (Jn. 15:11). The greatest mortification may be to accept and utilize for others all the gifts we have received. Christian spirituality then is concerned not with life-denying, but life-affirming: "I have come that you may have life and have it more abundantly" (Jn. 10:10).[30]

Consequently, the ascetico-mystical SanJuanist teachings are essentially rooted in the paschal mystery which underlines the mystical theology of the cross. For John, it is of chief importance that Christians would learn how to detach themselves from their egotistical desires by letting God be God in their lives. This spirit of detachment, of nakedness of spirit, is central for understanding the simple yet complicated formula that all works done for the love of God are good.

But, of course, killing infidels or heretics with a detached spirit is not the best way of praising the Lord. Following this example, one would think killing might be interpreted as leading the faithful to heaven. In that case,

---

[29] Ibid.

[30] Dyckman and Carroll, *Inviting the Mystic, Supporting the Prophet*, 16.

the believer is still attached to the idea of receiving some kind of heavenly reward that seeks self-gratification. As John declares: "The one who walks in the love of God seeks neither gain nor reward, but seeks only to lose with the will all things and self for God; and this loss the lover judges to be a gain."[31] In a nutshell, this last passage encompasses the celebrated SanJuanist mystical theology of the No-thing and the All (*la nada y el todo*). And this No-thing is precisely the All because God is not a thing.

The preference for the mixed life, for a life of balance, is one of the key elements in the SanJuanist mystical theology often overlooked by his commentators. Philosophically, John combines the Platonist or Augustinian ideas of goodness, truth, justice and love with the Aristotelian or Thomistic virtues of compassion, benevolence and purity. John receives a great influence from Neoplatonism via Saint Augustine and Pseudo-Dionysius. For instance, John says:

> *They also seriously distract these souls from the highest recollection, a recollection that consists in concentrating all the faculties on the incomprehensible Good and withdrawing them from all apprehensible things, for these apprehensible things are not a good that is beyond comprehension.*[32]

Moreover, John praised ancient pagan philosophers, wise men, and rulers for they are capable of doing good works. John writes: "Also many of the ancients possessed numerous virtues and engaged in good works, and many Christians have them today and accomplish wonderful deeds."[33] Aristotelian ethics had a great influence in Thomistic philosophy and theology. John as a scholastic person borrows the philosophical language from them and uses it in his mystical theology for his own purposes. An example of that is the following quotation:

---

[31] John of the Cross, *The Collected Works*, 590; *Spiritual Canticle* 29.11.

[32] Ibid., 276; *Ascent* 3.4.2.

[33] Ibid., 317; *Ascent* 3.27.4.

> *Moral goods are the fourth kind in which the will can rejoice. By moral goods we mean: the virtues and their habits insofar as they are moral; the exercise of any of the virtues; the practice of the works of mercy; the observance of God's law; political prudence, and all the practices of good manners.*[34]

Theologically, John integrates contemplation and action, faith and works, charity and apostolic service. As John puts it in the *Ascent of Mount Carmel*:

> *We would have achieved nothing by purging the intellect and memory in order to ground them in the virtues of faith and hope had we neglected the purification of the will through charity, the third virtue. Through charity works done in faith are living works and have high value; without it they are worth nothing, as St. James affirms: Without works of charity, faith is dead [Jas. 2:20].*[35]

As it was mentioned earlier in John's life, his faith grew stronger because he was deeply involved in doing works of charity as a labor of love. John always set priorities in the manner of his Jesuit fellow man, St. Ignatius of Loyola, who was famous for saying, "First things first." John did not forsake those who were in need of material or spiritual nourishment. He often helped those who were sick, hungry, thirsty, as Jesus did. John puts it this way,

> *all heavenly visions, revelations, and feelings . . . are not worth as much as the least act of humility. Humility has the effects of charity. It neither esteems nor seeks its own, it thinks no evil save of self, it thinks no good of self but of others. Consequently, souls should not look for their happiness in these supernatural apprehensions, but should strive to forget them for the sake of being free.*[36]

In other words, what kind of benefit would human souls receive if they pray constantly in their monastic cells or religious edifices without

---

[34] Ibid., 316; *Ascent* 3.27.1.

[35] Ibid., 291-292; *Ascent* 3.16.1.

[36] Ibid., 282; *Ascent* 3.9.4.

attending those who are in need? Are they really imitating Christ? John answers those questions by stating: "The will should rejoice only in what is for the honor and glory of God, and the greatest honor we can give him is to serve him according to evangelical perfection; anything unincluded in such service is without value to human beings."[37]

John the mystical theologian often justifies his thoughts by quoting from biblical passages. On this important matter of faith and charity John states: Serving God through them with true charity, for in charity lies the fruit of eternal life."[38] Thus, for John, faith without acts of virtue and love is blind and dead.

John, following the Ignatian dictum that "God can be found in all things," stresses the importance of ordinary, simple actions. In doing so, John acknowledges the mysterious presence of God in all things. John believes that the divine is reflected in all things, and all things are reflections of the divine only if one is aware of this mutual relationship. No matter if one is doing business, painting, singing, dancing, writing, or anything else, the Carmelite mystic becomes aware of the divine presence in all things. As John points out:

The soul goes about so solicitously on this step that it looks for its Beloved in all things. In all its thoughts it turns immediately to the Beloved; in all converse and business it at once speaks about the Beloved; when eating, sleeping, keeping vigil, or doing anything else, it centers all its care on the Beloved.[39]

---

[37] Ibid., 294; *Ascent* 3.17.2.

[38] Ibid., 324; *Ascent* 3.30.5.

[39] Ibid., 441; *Dark Night* 2.19.2. John also talks about how to practice the presence of God in all things as he told a religious friar how to reach perfection. John says:

You should consequently strive to be incessant in prayer, and in the midst of your corporeal practices do not abandon it. Whether you eat, or drink, or speak, or converse with lay people, or do anything else, you should always do so with desire for God and with your heart fixed on him. This is very necessary for inner solitude, which demands that the soul dismiss any thought that is not directed to God (*Counsels* 9).

John is well rooted in the Pauline message of 1 Cor. 15:28 and the long Christian mystical tradition that cherishes and nourishes the contemplative life. However, John does not see the contemplative life as superior to the active life. As it has been said before, faith without charity is dead. In the *Spiritual Canticle*, John traces the method in which the human soul seeks God. He writes:

> *And accordingly, in this third stanza she says that she herself through works desires to look for him, and she describes the method to be employed in order to find him: She must practice the virtues and engage in the spiritual exercises of both the active and the contemplative life. As a result she must tolerate no delights or comforts, and the powers and snares of her three enemies (the world, the devil, and the flesh) must neither detain nor impede her ... She points out here that for the attainment of God it is not enough to pray with the heart and the tongue or receive favors from others, but that together with this a soul must through its own effort do everything possible. God usually esteems the work persons do by themselves more than many other works done for them.*[40]

This passage indicates that John is not finding God in the contemplative life alone. To seek God through works is as important as praying within a monastic cell. John brings together the contemplative and the active life. Any action becomes a vehicle for God, if it imbedded in that spirit of complete surrender to God, without expecting any gain or reward.

In the past, scholars attributed to John quietistic elements. But as I have shown that is far from the truth. John combined contemplative practices with acts of virtue. To him, contemplation alone does not suffice without performing the necessary works of charity. The spiritual seeker must do something to find God. By practicing meditation and interior recollection, the Carmelites fulfill their spiritual vocation in the midst of the world.

---

[40] Ibid., 490; *Spiritual Canticle* 3.1-2.

John was well aware that the road to God was not easy. There are many barriers that impede the human soul from reaching his or her full potential. But God is present all the way. Out of great labor is born the virtuous person. As Aristotle says, virtue is a disposition of the human soul, a habit. For John, "the way to look for God is to do good works for him and mortify evil within oneself."[41]

---

[41] Ibid., 491; *Spiritual Canticle* 3.4.

4

THE MYSTICAL PATH OF WISDOM

"Allí me dio su pecho,
allí me enseñó ciencia muy sabrosa."
(poem from the *Spiritual Canticle*)

"There [Wisdom] gave me her breast,
there she revealed delightful knowledge to me."
(My own translation)

The "soul" is the intellectual capacity of human beings "to know, to study, to grapple with things and problems, to discuss, to have 'dialogue,' to decipher the mystery of reality."[1] The metaphor of the "soul" is associated with the Hindu mystical path of *jñāna yoga* which recognizes in each human being the possibility of contemplating through an intuitive understanding the "ontological awareness of all that is."[2] Intellectual mystics seek salvation through an experiential knowledge of the ultimate reality, the supreme being, the Godhead. This is what Robert Neville calls the path of the "sage." For Panikkar, the symbol that best represents the path of intellect is the element of water. In the SanJuanist index the word "water" is cited 180 times.[3] St. Teresa's favorite element was water.

---

[1] Panikkar, *Worship and Secular Man*, 87.

[2] Ibid.

[3] Astigarraga, Borrell, and Martín, *Concordancias*, 54-56.

Historically, John stood between the Middle Ages and the Renaisssance. Many commentators saw him as a medieval scholastic thinker devoid of any interest in the real world. Leonard Doohan suggests that although John was

> [r]ecognized as an intelligent student in his early years in Medina del Campo and Salamanca, he was later appreciated as a fine scholar by university faculties, at Baeza and elsewhere. However, he was not valued as an original thinker in his own day. In fact, theological originality was hardly what post-reformation Spain was looking for! John was usually considered a disciple of Thomas Aquinas and of the Aeropagite.[4]

Although John has been also portrayed as a Baroque religious thinker, I would argue that the Carmelite saint was a Renaissance man. John was truly imbedded in the Christian humanist tradition. Cardinal Cisneros created the University of Alcalá de Henares in 1499. The thinking of Erasmus of Rotterdam was in the air. And John was breathing that air. Later, he became rector of the Carmelite house of studies in Alcalá and Baeza. By embracing the principles of Christian humanism, John adopted a worldview already present in other European universities and monastic centers, thus advancing the Renaissance philosophy in Castile. Few people had received a humanistic education as John did at the University of Salamanca.

One of the central intellectual themes in John's mystical treatises is the need to explain the intrinsic relationship between experiential or living faith and philosophical [intuitive] reason. As Evelyn Underhill admits: "Often the true mystic is also a mystical philosopher; though there are plenty of mystical philosophers who are not and could never be mystics."[5]

A further commentary on the relation between mysticism and philosophy is exposed by W.T. Stace who states that "[m]ystics themselves

---

[4] Doohan, *The Contemporary Challenge of John of the Cross*, 5.

[5] Evelyn Underhill, *Mysticism* (New York: The New American Library, 1974), 95.

philosophize. In doing so they descend to the intellectual plane and therefore cannot expect to escape from intellectual criticism and analysis."[6] Furthermore, Stace asserts that "the question has to be raised whether we are bound thus to accept blindly and without criticism whatever report the mystic gives us of his experience."[7]

John's mystical theology is better understood in terms of the medieval mind which does not divorce *ratio* (the rational faculty of the human soul) from *intellectus* (the higher capacity of the intellect to grasp intuitively the divine). John was well rooted in the Thomistic scholastic tradition. In the words of researcher Manuela Dunn Mascetti:

> *In his Summa Theologica, Thomas Aquinas speaks of two kinds of knowledge – the knowledge derived from scientific inquiry or perfect use of reason and the knowledge derived from what he calls "connaturality," from the experience of "co-naturing," being in "co-presence" with an object, penetrating its essence intimately so that the object becomes embodied in oneself. We can test these two kinds of knowledge in our own lives.*[8]

John defines the human faculty of the intellect as *ratio* in the following passage:

> *Nothing in this life that could be imagined or received and understood by the intellect can be a proximate means of union with God. In our natural way of knowing, the intellect can grasp an object only through the forms and phantasms of things perceived by the bodily senses. Since, as we said, these things cannot serve as means, the intellect cannot profit from its natural knowing.*[9]

---

[6] W.T. Stace, *Mysticism and Philosophy* (Los Angeles: Jeremy P. Tarcher, 1960), 21-22.

[7] Ibid., 128.

[8] Manuela Dunn Mascetti, *Christian Mysticism* (New York: Hyperion, 1998), 135.

[9] John of the Cross, *The Collected Works*, 175; *Ascent* 2.8.4. In later chapters John clearly defines *ratio* as natural knowledge which "includes everything the intellect can understand by way of the bodily senses or through reflection" (*Ascent* 2.10.2).

By *intellectus* John means the following:

> *If we speak of supernatural knowing, insofar as one can in this life, we must say that the intellect of its ordinary power, while in the prison of this body, is neither capable of nor prepared for the reception of the clear knowledge of God. Such knowledge does not belong to our earthly state; either one must die or go without this knowledge.*[10]

For the Christian apophatic tradition, God is a *deus absconditus*, a hidden God who conceals, and yet reveals "Himself" in the created world as it is reported by mystics. The divine revelations (or theophanies) expressed by the mystics are usually accompanied by a symbolic and metaphorical language of fire and cloud.

In the Old Testament, Moses enters into the cloud alone leaving the multitude behind (Exodus 20:21). Moses' personal encounter with God "face to face" (Exodus 33:11) on Mount Horeb was with a God who hides "Himself" from the human eyes under the fire of the burning bush. This is the God of Abraham, Isaac, and Jacob. God's name is revealed as "I am who I am" (Exodus 3:14). And at the same time, God is concealed because the divine transcends the senses and the mind. That is why God reveals

---

[10] Ibid; *Ascent* 2.10.2. John also calls *intellectus* supernatural knowledge because it "comprises everything imparted to the intellect in a way transcending the intellect's natural ability and capacity." Later, John explains the relationship between *intellectus* and *ratio* by saying:

> *The spiritual light has a similar relationship to the intellect, the eye of the soul. This supernatural general knowledge and light shines so purely and simply in the intellect and is so divested and freed of all intelligible forms (the objects of the intellect) that it is imperceptible to the soul. This knowledge, when purer, is even at times the cause of darkness because it dispossesses the intellect of its customary lights, forms, and phantasies and effects a noticeable darkness (John of the Cross, The Collected Works, 194-195; Ascent 2.14.10).*

John is referring to the contemplative state in which the human soul and the intellect are blinded or suspended for a short period of time so that God infuses a loving, delightful knowledge to the soul in darkness. Thus, Christian contemplatives often put into practice the spiritual discipline of total surrender of senses and intelligible forms before God so that the practitioner prepares himself or herself to a certain degree for encountering the luminous darkness within.

"Himself" under the fire of the burning bush or perhaps why Moses can see only God's back (Exodus 33:18-20).

Moses never saw God with his physical eyes but rather with "the inner eye of love" (using William Johnston's words). There is no anthropomorphic face to see in Moses' encounter with God because no human being has ever seen God's face. God is not an object among other objects. The Old Testament says: "You cannot see my face; for man shall not see me and live" (Ex. 33:20). Moses had hidden his face before, "for he was afraid to look at God" (Ex. 3:6). As Deirdre Carabine states: "Thus, even the experience of God's intimate friend is an experience of divine hiddenness. Although God's presence is strongly perceived by his chosen people, he never reveals his true nature to them; he remains *deus absconditus*."[11]

The archetypical figure of Moses becomes a model for the apophatic mystics. The No-thingness of God will become a recurrent theme in the Christian mystical tradition, especially in the works of Gregory of Nyssa and Dionysius, and later in the anonymous author of *The Cloud of the Unknowing* and in St. John of the Cross.

Let me digress for a moment and turn to the study of Neoplatonic ideas in the Christian mystics. Some important contemporary scholars either have denied altogether the Neoplatonic influence on the Christian mystical tradition or have affirmed the Neoplatonic presence in Christian mysticism only as a denigrating aspect that still today has not yet been overcome. According to Harvey Egan, the latter authors are:

> *Karl Barth, Emil Brunner, Friedrich Heiler, Albrecht Ritschl, Nathan Söderblom, Ernst Troeltsch, and Adolf Harnack ... [who] reject the longstanding Christian mystical tradition as a pagan, neo-Platonic*

---

[11] Deirdre Carabine, *The Unknown God. Negative Theology in the Platonic Tradition: Plato to Eriugena* (Louvain, Belgium: Peeters Press, 1995), 201.

infection and deformation of Christianity, or as Roman Catholic piety in an extreme form.[12]

However, clearly Christian mysticism borrows from Neoplatonism its language and philosophy, and John's mysticism is a product of that hybrid version of pagan and Christian influences. St. Augustine and St. Thomas Aquinas are perfect exemplars of the same kind of creative synthesis achieved in medieval Christianity.

It is unfortunate that religious and non-religious thinkers still, today, make the distinction between the Christian God and the God of the philosophers (if they have any God at all). Adolf von Harnack thought that the Christian dogmas had departed from the Gospels since he recognized the great impact of Hellenistic ideas in the third and fourth century. Harnack proposed to get rid of the Hellenistic ideas in Christianity by using his historical critical method alone to recover the true Christian spirit of the Gospels. Other historians of doctrine like A.J. Festugière held the view that the Greek Fathers were Platonizing Christianity. However, Festugière did not completely disregard Hellenism, although he saw it as an independent tradition.

---

[12] Harvey D. Egan, *An Anthology of Christian Mysticism* (Collegeville, Minnesota: The Liturgical Press, 1996), xxv. However, Egan believes that "mysticism cannot be reconciled with biblical, prophetic religion and that Christian mysticism is a neo-Platonic distortion of genuine biblical Christianity." He further says that

> *the real ancestry of Christian mysticism is not to be found in the influence of Greek philosophy, but in the Bible. The 'origins of the Christian mystical tradition' are first and foremost in Scripture, not in neo-Platonism. Although the Christian mystical tradition was enriched by neo-Platonism and is being enriched in our time by Eastern religions, authentic Christian mysticism looks to the solidly mystical spirituality of the New Testament and Jesus' trinitarian mystical consciousness that reached its high point in his salvific death and resurrection. And both Jesus' mystical consciousness and New Testament mysticism in general cannot be understood without a knowledge of Old Testament mysticism (pp. 13-14).*

However, I disagree with Harvey Egan's statement of the superiority of the Catholic truth over any other tradition. Rather, I think that Neoplatonic thinking not only enriches Christian mysticism but also serves the purpose of establishing the foundations of its mystical language.

A careful reading of the major philosophical treatises available in the Hellenistic Christian world might lead one to conclude that there is no radical separation between philosophy and religion as such. According to Deirdre Carabine, "Neoplatonism itself was not simply a philosophical system; it was also a way of life."[13]

Historically, the word "mysticism" or "mystery" is associated with the Greek mystery religions which flourished in the sixth century before the common era. Eleusian, Dionysian, Orphic, and Pythagorean cults gained many devotees. There were initiatory rites and ceremonies in these esoteric circles that are oriented to help the devotee to achieve union with the divine. The hierarchical orders persuaded and even imposed on the initiated to keep their mouths shut ("*muein*") so that they could remain silent (without sharing any of their personal experiences), and perhaps in so doing they could avoid persecutions.

Neoplatonism was to inherit the legacy of the Greek mystery religions, but the Neoplatonists appropriated the esoteric language to create a new method for preparing the way to what Christians called later meditative practices. The Neoplatonists attempted to flee from the world, to shut their eyes from all multiplicity and all externality, so that they could ascend to the One. The Neoplatonic mystics developed a philosophical doctrine concerning the nature of the One (or the Godhead), the relation of the "alone with the Alone" (or the human soul and God), and the human soul's ascent into God. Plotinus shaped the mystical philosophy outside of the Christian tradition. His description of the mystical ascent to the heavenly realms profoundly marked the Christian mystical language, especially that of Dionysius, Bonaventure, and of course, St. John of the Cross.

Plotinus was also important because he stressed the mystical path of wisdom (or Christ as the divine *Logos*), which had a tremendous impact in the Patristic period among Origen, Gregory of Nyssa (Basil's brother), and Dionysius the Areopagite; and later, among St. Augustine, St. Bonaventure,

---

[13] Carabine, *The Unknown God*, x.

the Rhineland mystics, and St. John of the Cross. Thus, the mystical path is no longer understood as a mysticism of action or of devotion alone but now there is room for a mysticism of the intellect.

Mystical speculation was also conceived as a way of life, for the ascent to the One is an existential journey through the intellect, not merely through reason alone. The higher faculty of the intellect has also an affective and an active part to play in the mystical path. Therefore, the Neoplatonists might have achieved a creative synthesis between the body (through meditative and purgative exercises), the mind (through speculative reflections), and the heart (through ecstasy).

It has also been demonstrated that there was a Hellenizing of Judaic sources and themes in the works of Philo of Alexandria, a Jewish philosopher of the first century. Philo's genius and uniqueness lie in his ability to synthesize the most important thoughts of the Platonic and Hebraic doctrines. Philo had a great influence on Christianity and on the Christian mystics because of his doctrine of the *Logos*, the Son of God, and his allegorical interpretations of the Scriptures.

The Cappadocian fathers' doctrine of the incomprehensibility and ineffability of God was developed in the fourth century particularly by Gregory of Nyssa's mystical theology. He knew from his personal experience that God is "the holy of holies," "the mystery of mysteries," who likes to hide "Himself." No one has ever seen God's face because there is no such face to be seen. What human beings can know about God is through a loving knowledge, an immediate direct encounter with the mystery of God's Trinity, where the human soul feels God's presence at the deepest center of his or her soul. William Johnston declares:

> *And Gregory of Nyssa in his Life of Moses appeals to the example of the great Hebrew lawgiver climbing the mountain and entering the cloud of darkness. Moses left everything, even thinking, to enter into the*

unknowing and to meet God. And there is no other way in which the human can meet the divine.[14]

Gregory of Nyssa's influence on Dionysius and later on St. John of the Cross is as important as that of *Exodus*. The archetypical figure of Moses in his ascent to the summit of the mountain and entering into the cloud of unknowing will play a central role in the history of Christian mysticism from now on.

Christian theologians owe a great deal to the Greek Fathers (especially to Clement of Alexandria and Irenaeus, Gregory of Nyssa and Augustine) for having preserved and transmitted the Neoplatonic heritage, and in particular, for adopting their mystical philosophy as the solid foundation for the future of the Christian mystical theology.

Dionysius the Aeropagite would become the bridge between Neoplatonist and Christian mystics. According to modern scholars, Dionysius was a Syrian monk, a Christian Neoplatonist influenced by Proclus and the Greek Fathers, who probably lived at the end of the fifth century or the beginning of the sixth century. William Johnston recorded the great influence that Dionysius had in the Christian mystical writings. Johnston summarizes the list of names in the following order:

> *Bonaventure calls Dionysius the prince of mystics; Thomas Aquinas quotes him some seventeen hundred times; Dante sings the praises of the Aeropagite. His Mystical Theology strongly influenced the apophatic mystical tradition from Eckhart and Tauler to St. John of the Cross and on to this very day. The author of the Cloud of the Unknowing considered him so important that he made a free translation--it may well be called an adaptation--entitled Deonise Hid Divinite.*[15]

---

[14] William Johnston, *Mystical Theology: The Science of Love* (London: HarperCollins Publishers, 1995), 19.

[15] Ibid., 20.

St. John of the Cross quotes Dionysius the Aeropagite only four times in his writings; however, John gives Dionysius full credit for having built the pillars of mystical theology, also known as "the science of love." Moreover, John, in his intellectual capacities creatively combines Neoplatonism with Aristotelian or Thomistic thinking. His apparent dualism between earthly and heavenly knowledge is not inclined to despise or reject the world as such; on the contrary, John construes his philosophical or theological distinctions on purely abstract concepts following the Neoplatonist-Thomistic metaphysical categories and their epistemological frameworks.

Additionally, while John uses Aquinas's metaphysics and epistemology in his commentaries by stressing the idea that knowledge comes first through the senses (or through the material or created world), John clearly adheres to the Neoplatonist-Augustinian philosophy. John, like Plotinus or St. Augustine, claims that ultimately the human mind as *ratio* cannot know God's essence by discursive, analytical, or deductive reasoning alone. Something else is perhaps needed in order to know God fully. Or, as John suggests in the *Ascent*, the process of acquiring knowledge seems to follow the next steps:

Since the order followed in the process of knowing involves the forms and images of created things, and since knowledge is acquired through the senses, God, to achieve his work gently and to lift the soul to supreme knowledge, must begin by touching the low state and extreme of the senses. And from there he must gradually bring the soul after its own manner to the other end, spiritual wisdom, which is incomprehensible to the senses. Thus, naturally or supernaturally, he brings people to his supreme spirit by first instructing them through discursive meditation and through forms, images, and sensible means, according to their own manner of coming to understand.[16]

John gives priority to mystical intuition over discursive reasoning without denying the importance of the role that rational discernment plays in the

---

[16] John of the Cross, *The Collected Works*, 206; *Ascent* 2.17.3.

process of understanding ultimate reality. In other words, John follows the scholastic theologians (especially St. Anselm of Canterbury and St. Thomas Aquinas) in suggesting that faith (or the obscure knowledge of God) seeks understanding so that the blessed soul will comprehend the incomprehensible. Yet Aquinas never claims that the human mind can ever know God by a deductive rational method alone. In that sense, Aquinas follows St. Augustine and the long Christian mystical tradition in acknowledging the impossibility of knowing God by reason alone.

For John, human knowledge is "unlike and disproportioned to God['s knowledge]."[17] However, John believes human beings can reach union with God in this life not merely by human effort or by rational analysis, but ultimately by letting God be God at the apex of the human soul. Most mystical theologians agree with John that God infuses divine knowledge to the higher faculty of the human intellect (namely, the *intellectus*). And this contemplative mode of knowing requires a type of person who is receptive to God's grace. Nonetheless, John does not advocate for a type of passivity that annuls a human response to God's grace. On the contrary, John is well aware of the urgent task that human beings are called to undertake (especially those who have been blessed) in building the kingdom of God on earth.

Clearly, John follows the apophatic mystical tradition by negating all that is not God. Apophatic mystics or theologians reject the possibility that the human intellect alone can reach union with God because human reason cannot serve as "a proportionate means to the attainment of God."[18]

---

[17] Ibid., 175; *Ascent* 2.8.5.

[18] Ibid., 174; *Ascent* 2.8.3. John borrows from Aristotle and Aquinas the philosophical argument that "all means must be proportionate to their end" (Aristotle, *Metaphysics* 2.1; Aquinas, *Summa theologiae* 1-2.96.1; 1-2.102.1; 1, 2.114.2.). Furthermore, John believes that the human intellect cannot reach union with God without the help of God's grace. Therefore, John concludes that the human intellect alone does not bear a likeness to God's essence. He truly thinks that there is an infinite gap between God and the human intellect that can only be bridged by the gift of grace. And this gift cannot be verified in the philosophical domain because it transcends reason. In fact, John says that faith alone "is the only proximate and

Paradoxically, John is also a cataphatic mystic. He is fond of affirming God's attributes (light, flame, love, and so forth). John reveals how the mystic is able to know God's glory in this life by a simple act of grace, which is infused in the human soul. And this higher knowledge called infused contemplation, mystical theology, contemplation, dark night, faith, or divine wisdom is accessible through the passive intellect called *intellectus*. John defines it as

> *[c]ontemplation, consequently, by which the intellect has a higher knowledge of God, is called mystical theology, meaning the secret wisdom of God. For this wisdom is secret to the very intellect that receives it. St. Dionysius on this account refers to contemplation as a ray of darkness. The prophet Baruch declares of this wisdom: There is no one who knows her way or can think of her paths [Bar. 3:23]. To reach union with God the intellect must obviously blind itself to all the paths along which it can travel.*[19]

Thus, St. John of the Cross does not write his mystical writings in isolation from his religious and cultural environment. Rather, the Carmelite writer needs to be seen in the light of a continuous line of mystical thoughts that are primarily rooted in the Judeo-Christian biblical tradition, and yet not completely deprived of other possible influences coming from the non-Christian world (particularly the Greek, Latin, Jewish and Muslim traditions).

John is versed in the study of the Bible and often quotes from the Gospels to support his theological arguments. The Carmelite saint truly exemplifies the Johannine spirit, especially relying heavily on the theological virtues of love and faith put into action, when the Evangelist says, "Dear children, let us put our love not into words or into talk but into deeds, and make it real" (I John 3:16-18).

---

proportionate means [to the intellect] to union with God [by love]" (John of the Cross, *The Collected Works*, 177; *Ascent* 2.9.1).

[19] Ibid., 176; *Ascent* 2.8.6.

St. John of the Cross is a mystical theologian who reformulates for us the long Christian mystical tradition of the Desert Fathers, Pseudo-Dionysius, and all the other saints, sages, mystics, and prophets. John not only writes about mysticism as a theologian, but he also articulates his thoughts out of his deep, personal union with the divine. The Carmelite saint does not divorce mysticism from theology, *intellectus* from *ratio*, experiential faith from reason.

It seems that John is closer in his thoughts to the Orthodox Christian tradition, especially dealing with his mystical theology and the concept of *theosis*, or divinization. For John, the mystical experience must be always accompanied by theological explanations. The Carmelite accomplishes his mystical task through his poetry and prose commentaries. Manuela Dunn Mascetti reports that

> *The early twentieth century Russian theologian Vladimir Lossky affirmed that the Eastern tradition has never made a sharp distinction between mysticism and theology when he declared, "There is no Christian mysticism without theology; but, above all, there is no theology without mysticism ... Mysticism is the perfecting and crown of all theology: it is theology par excellence."*[20]

Scholars agree that one of John's most significant intellectual contributions is his mixture of mystical poetry and theological commentaries in his writings. John's mystical poetry centers around the Christian paschal mystery of death (*kenosis*) and resurrection (*pleroma*) using those two theological themes as pivotal images in the *Ascent to Mt. Carmel* and in the *Dark Night of the Soul*: "I abandoned and forgot myself" (*kenosis*) and "laying my face on my Beloved" (*pleroma*). Likewise, St. John of the Cross identifies the kenotic movement with *la nada* and the pleromatization process with *el todo*.

There are a great number of researchers (among them Asín Palacios, López-Baralt, Annemarie Schimmel, Cuevas García, and Satz) who drew

---

[20] Mascetti, *Christian Mysticism*, 156.

from their investigations certain parallels between John's mystical poetry and Sufism, based primarily on their shared usage of mystical symbols.

For instance, John frequently makes use of such expressions as "the wine of mystical intoxication," which stands for mystical ecstasy; the symbol of the "dark night of the soul;" the "lamps of fire that illuminate the ecstatic soul;" the "solitary bird of the soul in ecstatic flight;" and the image of "dying before you die." These expressions are essential for understanding his spiritual theology of detachment (*kenosis/nada*) and rest in the divine (*pleroma/todo*), which echoes the Sufi teaching of *fana-wa-baqa*. All in all, the Sufis had employed to some degree the SanJuanist mystical expressions mentioned above, even centuries earlier.

The real question is, then, did John borrow certain symbols and expressions from the Sufi tradition? And if so, why? Or better said, could it be that mystics from all cultures and times share their rich symbols without giving proper credit to their respective cultural and religious heritages? Most mystics claim that the source of mystical inspiration is the same for all, regardless of their cultural and religious differences.

It is not an exaggeration to affirm that the Carmelite saint felt at home using Muslim, Jewish, and Christian symbolic expressions. Three reasons come to mind: first, the Iberian Peninsula was historically influenced by the three monotheistic religions of the West, even after the expulsion of the Jews in the fifteenth century and the Moors (or *moriscos*) in the seventeenth century; second, John not only had access to the best university libraries in the kingdom of Castile (Salamanca, Alcalá de Henares, and Baeza), but he also knew people who were knowledgeable or in contact with non-Christian sources; and third, John himself could have been raised in a Jewish and Moorish household if it is accepted the theory that his parents were *conversos*.

According to Asín Palacios, a great number of connections between John and the Muslim world can be made based on the hypothesis of literary transmission by *moriscos*. He writes:

> *This comparison of texts with parallels in ideas and technical metaphors could be extended to other aspects of the asceticism and mysticism of both schools, the Shadhilite and the Carmelite ... A large number of Moriscos recently converted to Christianity lived throughout Spain, not only in Andalusia but also in Castile. It is not to be believed that with their conversion they would have forgotten their Islamic education, especially in those subjects common to both religions and not pertaining to dogma, that is to say, in all that refers to asceticism and mysticism.*
>
> *In all the cities and villages that were the scenes of the life of Saint John of the Cross – Arévalo, Medina, Pastrana, Salamanca, Granada, Alcalá, Segovia, Ávila, and Toledo--the statistics of the seventeenth century reveal that even then there existed many nuclei of Moriscos. The royal decrees of expulsion excepted from banishment the clergy and the members of religious orders of both sexes who were registered as new Christians, that is, converted Moriscos. There would undoubtedly be others among the illuminati (enlightened) of Andalusia and Castile. The processes of inquisition, explored with this purpose, would help to clear up the problem.*[21]

It is not surprising, then, to view John's constant persecutions, fears and apparent silence in light of his social background, that of being a new Christian. Could it be possible that Doria and some inquisitors knew about John's social stigma, namely being a descendant from a *morisco* and/or a *marrano* (Jewish *converso*)? Why did some Carmelite brothers put John in prison? Why did they also try to expel him from the Discalced Carmelite Order if he was the co-founder with Teresa of this monastic tradition? Why did Doria want to send John to Mexico months before his death? Why did the manuscripts suffer so many revisions? Why did it take so long to beatify, canonize, and elect him the Mystical Doctor of the Church?

---

[21] Miguel Asín Palacios, *Saint John of the Cross and Islam*, trans. Howard W. Yoder and Elmer H. Douglas (New York: Vantage Press, 1981), 28-29.

The answer to all those questions could be found in St. John of the Cross's lineage. This alone could explain some of the reasons behind John's apparent silence and the fear of being persecuted by inquisitors. Witnesses have reported that most of John's letters were burned for the fear of being put in the hands of the Inquisition. Why fear? Anything to hide?

Although there is no established evidence that John ever had any direct contact with Sufism, he was, without any doubt, influenced by the Moorish legacy in the Iberian Peninsula. John probably knew some members of the Muslim communities in Granada. The *morisco* population in Granada was high even in the sixteenth century. *Moriscos* had preserved the Islamic culture and faith in the neighborhood of El Albaicín. Besides that, John lived in a historical site once occupied by the Moors. Christians were kept as prisoners in that desert land, thereby giving the region its adopted name: los Mártires (the Martyrs). Later this area became known as the site for the Discalced Carmelite friars in Granada.

John held the position of prior of the Monastery of los Mártires for more than six years. The monastery was located across from the Alhambra, the last Muslim bastion in the Iberian Peninsula. The palace and its gardens, even today, display through art and architecture the religious interface that took place between Christianity and Islam during several centuries of coexistence. John felt at home in Granada. Proof of that is the number of writings (most of his commentaries and poems were written in Granada) and activities undertook between 1582 and 1588.

John embraces in his mystical poetry and, above all, in his mystical theology, the double movement of *la nada* and *el todo*. The Sufi mystical teaching of *fana-wa-baqa* fits into the SanJuanist description of *la nada y el todo*. *Fana*, or annihilation of the soul in Allah, corresponds to *la nada*. And *baqa*, or subsistence in God, is the equivalent of *el todo*. Similarly, John states: the divine fire will "never kill unless to give life, never wound unless to heal."[22] By God's grace, the human soul reaches union with God in this life. But in

---

[22] John of the Cross, *The Collected Works*, 663; *Living Flame of Love* 2.16.

order to reach the highest union with the divine in this life, the human soul must learn how to detach himself or herself from all egotistical desires and vicious habits so that the human soul is consumed in God's glory.

In the *Living Flame of Love*, John distinguishes between the old self and the new self in God by giving some thoughts to his mystical poetry: "in killing you changed death to life." John declares that "the soul is unable to live perfectly in this new life if the old self does not die completely."[23] Undoubtedly, John associates the old self with those bad habits that must be reordered (perhaps owing to the medieval monastic definition of sin) in order to find new life in God. By undergoing such personal transformations, the human soul might be able to let God change the spiritual state from "death to life." John writes: "Consequently the soul is dead to all it was in itself, which was death to it, and alive to that God is in himself."[24]

St. Teresa of Ávila also writes about this double movement between detachment from all egotistical desires and attachment to the divine life. Teresa argues that the idea of detachment (or "interior mortification") has little or nothing to do with bodily penances. For Teresa, true detachment can only be achieved when the human soul surrenders to God's will. Subsequently, Teresa shares John's theological explanations of the double movement in the mystical life by acknowledging the following: "His Majesty must place us there and enter Himself into the center of the soul,"[25] although "[t]rue union can very well be reached, with God's help, if we make the effort to obtain it by keeping our wills fixed only on that which is God's will."[26]

---

[23] Ibid., 670; *Living Flame of Love*, 2.33.

[24] Ibid., 671; *Living Flame of Love*, 2.34.

[25] Teresa of Avila, *The Collected Works of St. Teresa of Avila*, ed. Kieran Kavanaugh and Otilio Rodríguez (Washington, District of Columbia: ICS Publications, 1980), 340; *Interior Castle* V:1.12.

[26] Ibid., 349; *Interior Castle* V:3.2.

Teresa's notion of detachment "is like one who in every respect has died to the world so as to live more completely in love."[27] There is no doubt in my mind that Teresa shapes and influences John's mystical theology in many ways, especially in regard to the central teaching of getting rid of our egotistical desires and of "our attachment to any earthly thing."[28] In the Sufi tradition, they say that the self must "die before he or she dies." There might be certain parallels between the Sufi experience and Teresa's own mystical experience when she asserts that the devoted soul "would want to dissolve and die a thousand deaths for Him."[29]

John's mystical theology borrows from the Christian mystical tradition the two mystical states of contemplation, namely acquired and infused. The former state requires human effort with the aid of God's grace so that the soul can be prepared to receive the seeds of contemplation planted by God in the human soul; the latter state that of infused contemplation which is the pure gift of God.

Christian mystics share the belief that by letting our egotistical desires die we die to ourselves and subsequently we are reborn even in this life as new beings in Christ. Asceticism, often associated by Christians with the purgative way, emblematizes to a certain degree the death of our egotistical or unhealthy desires by stressing the acquired contemplation mode. This mode alone does not guarantee a mystical experience but at least it prepares the ground for the illuminative and unitive states of the mystical life. On the other hand, mysticism represents the culmination of the spiritual journey by associating itself with the illuminative and unitive ways. The human soul is transformed into God by participation or "*a lo divino*," as John puts it. At this point, God infuses divine knowledge and loving wisdom to the blessed soul. Hence, asceticism and mysticism form an integral part of the Christian life.

---

[27] Ibid., 336; *Interior Castle* V:1.4.

[28] Ibid., 343; *Interior Castle* V:2.6.

[29] Ibid., 344; *Interior Castle* V:2.7.

Also, John's mystical theology develops a twofold "dialectical" movement: on the one hand, John follows the spiritual practice of letting go (*kenosis*); and on the other hand, John allows God to be God in us (*pleroma*). The former path is also known as the apophatic way (or the *via negativa*), by which one affirms by way of negation and by radically detaching from all that obstructs the human soul to reach out to the divine so that the soul is totally naked before God in faith. The latter path is known as the cataphatic way (or the *via positiva*), by virtue of which one affirms God's attributes without undermining the essence of God's ineffable mystery which cannot ultimately be defined, although it can be experienced by the mystic.

St. John of the Cross is often called an apophatic mystic because of his radical doctrine of detachment. But the reality is somewhat different. In John, the apophatic (or the mysticism of darkness) and the cataphatic (or the mysticism of light) go hand in hand. The apophatic way is the way of negation by virtue of which the mystic explains the unexplainable; that is to say, by saying what God is not. John's famous concept of *la nada* illustrates his mystical doctrine of detachment. Conversely, the cataphatic way is the road of affirmation by virtue of which mystical theologians describe the attributes of the Godhead. For instance, John identifies the living flame of love with the divine life, or the mystery of the Godhead.

But why did John choose the image of the dark night as his own personal description of ultimate reality? The SanJuanist dark night of the soul has been interpreted in the past by readers and scholars alike as if John's soteriological teachings meant that one experience God without undergoing some measure of pain. By the same token, it might be difficult for some Christians to explain the mystery of the cross when this incarnational moment is being reduced to the suffering and pain of Jesus as the Christ during the crucifixion. But isn't the Christian teaching of the cross a mystery? In what ways did John use the mystical symbol of the dark night?

In regard to St. John of the Cross's ascetic life, Helmut A. Hatzfeld points out that the Carmelite saint "became famous especially because of his emphasis on the bitter periods in the mystical life, which he calls with an unforgettable symbol *La noche oscura del alma* (*The Dark Night of the Soul*)."[30] This symbol is often associated with strict asceticism, austerity, and suffering, perhaps linking John's extreme bodily asceticism and his imprisonment in Toledo to the persecution and tragic destiny of Jesus Christ who was crucified and died on the cross for the sins of humanity. Following a long devotional practice of imitating the life of Jesus Christ, John has been traditionally portrayed by hagiographers and by some SanJuanist commentators as another martyr. To illustrate this point, René Fülöp-Miller understood the experience of John's dark night in relation to his imprisonment in Toledo. René writes:

> *Then too, Teresa recovered also St. John of the Cross. He returned, steeled by the martyrdom of prison, transfigured in the eyes of all Christians by the miracle of his escape. The calced Carmelites, who had abducted him, kept him for nine months locked up in a narrow chamber inside the wall of one of their monasteries ... Night after night the flogging went on, but St. John of the Cross did not abjure ... for all this torture was for him but one of the stations of his imitatio Christi ... For it was a life that turned into song, into verse and stanza, and in it the torment he had suffered was changed into sweetness ... The tormentors were thinking of new forms of torture, but the stanzas of divine passion had been brought to perfection. A radiant vision penetrated the darkness of St. John's prison.*[31]

Even in the media, the symbol of the dark night is often associated with suffering and torment. On May 1, 1999, Bob Hohler writes in *The Boston Globe* an article entitled "Jackson prays with US soldiers held in Belgrade.

---

[30] Helmut A. Hatzfeld, *Santa Teresa de Ávila* (New York: Twayne Publishers, 1969), 141-142.

[31] René Fülöp-Miller, *The Saints that Moved the World* (New York: Collier Books, 1962), 466-477.

Seeks an end to 'dark night.'" The first sentence states: "They prayed for morning to come after their 'long, dark night' of captivity." Did Mr. Hohler rightly use the SanJuanist expression of the 'dark night' by comparing John's captivity in Toledo with those US soldiers held in Belgrade? Clearly not.

St. John of the Cross defines the dark night as "an inflow of God into the soul," which "the contemplatives call infused contemplation or mystical theology."[32] Thus John identifies the experience of the dark night with the unitive state of the mystical life by becoming the human soul God by participation. Paradoxically, the SanJuanist dark night is a glad night because the lover and the beloved are united and transformed by love in the night.

Perhaps it is necessary to pose the following question before I discuss in depth the SanJuanist symbol in relation to John's life and thoughts. Did John experience his famous 'dark night' while being captive in the prison of Toledo? Most certainly not. In 1577, John was abducted in Ávila and moved to Toledo, where he was shut up in a small cell inside the Discalced Carmelite monastery. He was accused of rebellion against the Carmelite Order. Most SanJuanist scholars agree that St. John of the Cross did not write the *Dark Night* while he was imprisoned. Instead, John redacted his poems of the *Spiritual Canticle*.

The SanJuanist symbol of the dark night should not be identified with pain and suffering alone (as many commentators do--especially theologians who read John's famous symbol as "the dark night of injustice") but rather with the highest degree of union with God that one can achieve in this life. Camilo Maccise puts it this way:

> *The teaching of St. John of the Cross is about the transformation of the human person in God. In this sense it is an illuminating and modern doctrine. It leads the human person to live to the fullest his or her status as a child of God. It introduces individuals to a new world of*

---

[32] John of the Cross, *The Collected Works*, 401; *Dark Night* 2.5.1.

relationships with God and creatures (III Ascent 20, 2; 23, 1; Flame 3, 7).[33]

Merton warns the reader of possible misreadings of John's mystical teachings. By removing him from his humanity, his concreteness, and his monastic tradition, John's theology can be dehumanized. Also, Merton suggests that we need to read John in light of the biblical tradition by following a long line of prophetic mystics who try to explain the unexplainable (namely, the death and resurrection of Christ).

John understands the symbol of the dark night not as a pure negation but rather as the highest expression of light, love, and truth that human beings can experience in this life. It is dark because there is no-thing to see. God is not an object. It is beyond any concept or vision whatsoever. In biblical terms, Moses in Exodus never claimed to see God's face because there was no face to see. The biblical passage from Exodus allegorically describes the presence that Moses felt at Mount Sinai referring to God's back as a symbol for the hiddenness of the Godhead. And the burning bush could be interpreted as a sign of the reality of God whose presence is manifested almost as an epiphany to Moses.

The SanJuanist doctrine of the dark night is often misrepresented and John is regarded as "a life-denying and world-hating ascetic, when in reality his mysticism super-abounds in love, vitality, and joy."[34] For some readers, the dark night means turning away from all created and sensible things so that you will come to know God, even at the expense of excluding fraternal union. For Thomas Merton, "this is bad theology and bad asceticism."[35] Actually, it is through this dark night that we can let God find us in total surrender by an act of grace. In other words, John's symbol of the dark

---

[33] Camilo Maccise, "John of the Cross and the New Evangelization," *Spiritual Life* 38:3 (1992): 164.

[34] Thomas Merton, *Zen and the Birds of Appetite* (New York: A New Directions Book, 1968), 81.

[35] Thomas Merton, *Contemplative Prayer* (New York: Image Books, 1990), 38.

night might be interpreted as absence of light in encountering the mystery of the Godhead. Yet the mystic receives infused knowledge from God's luminous revelations.

The mystical doctrine of the dark night not only teaches how the human soul prepares the way to encounter the divine through "privation and purgation of all sensible appetites for the external things of the world"[36] but also takes into account the actual encounter between God and the mystic by way of purgation, illumination, and union.

John's symbol of the dark night follows the double movement in mystical theology between acquired and infused contemplation. The SanJuanist dark night of the senses must be understood in the context of acquired contemplation by which human beings actively participate in the process of encountering God by human effort alone. The practitioner will make every effort to get rid of all egotistical desires by quieting the mind so that the human soul can rest in God; however, this process is not yet complete until the dark night of the spirit, understood by John to be the dark night of contemplation (that is, infused contemplation), takes place. God enters mysteriously and obscurely in the life of the contemplative by purifying one's self and in return the human soul responds to God's grace with thanksgiving and loving attention. In other words, it is God who now takes the initiative while the potential mystic prepares the way for the human-divine encounter in an act of complete surrender before God.

St. John of the Cross warns contemplatives of the dangers of confusing mystical or infused contemplation with secondary phenomena such as ecstasies, raptures, stigmata, and other supernatural events. These heavenly gifts are nonetheless the simple effects caused by God's seeds of contemplation planted at the deepest center of the human soul. John believes that the contemplative cannot reach God by his or her own human effort. Faith, for John, is the experiential mode of encountering the living God at the

---

[36] John of the Cross, *The Collected Works*, 119; *Ascent* 1.1.4.

apex of the human soul. John construes his notion of faith as a dark night to the senses and to the spirit.

John uses the image of the dark night as a sign of death to the egotistical desires and a sign of life and resurrection in this life. Thomas Merton correctly observes that

> [t]he purpose of the dark night, as St. John of the Cross shows, is not simply to punish and afflict the heart of man, but to liberate, to purify and to enlighten in perfect love. The way that leads through dread goes not to despair but to perfect joy, not to hell but to heaven.[37]

Ruth Burrow observes that the whole aim of St. John of the Cross is "to release us from the tyranny of the ego."[38] However, Constance FitzGerald adds that

> desire is not suppressed or destroyed but gradually transferred, purified, transformed, set on fire ... Dark night is instead [of a sign of death] a sign of life, of growth, of development in our relationship with God, in our best human relationships, in our societal life. It is a sign to move on in hope to a new vision, a new experience.[39]

The task of the Christian ascetic is to become poor in the spirit so that he or she can let God work in him or her. The practitioner moves from fragmentation to integration to personal wholeness. Consequently, John's symbol of the dark night represents death to egotistical desires and resurrection to the new life in God. Therefore, neither the senses, the imagination, the discursive thinking, the intuition alone can bring oneself closer to God, for "God supernaturally illumines the soul with the ray of his divine

---

[37] Thomas Merton, *The Climate of Monastic Prayer* (Kalamazoo, Michigan: Cistercian Publications, 1969), 148.

[38] Slattery, *The Springs of Carmel*, 76.

[39] Constance FitzGerald, "Impasse and Dark Night," in *Women's Spirituality* (New York: Paulist Press, 1986), 291.

light"⁴⁰ which is darkness to sense and reason; that is to say, the darkening ("*la nada*") coincides with the experience of enlightenment ("*el todo*").

In other words, the darkness itself is light, pure faith, for true contemplation is "nothing else than a secret and peaceful and loving inflow of God [into the soul], which, if not hampered, fires the soul in the spirit of love"⁴¹ purging it of its ignorances and imperfections.

Merton's understanding of John's mystical teachings of *la nada y el todo* in light of his radical doctrine of detachment is clear in his *Seeds of Contemplation*:

> *One of the greatest paradoxes of the mystical life is this: that a man cannot enter into the deepest center of himself and pass through that center into God, unless he is able to pass entirely out of himself and empty himself and give himself to other people in the purity of a selfless love.*⁴²

The paradoxical nature of the mystical experience is at the heart of Christianity which is particularly confined to the central meaning of the cross. Perhaps John adopted his religious name (Juan de la Cruz) after grasping the true, hidden meaning of the Christian symbol of the cross. If John was marked by the sign of the cross, one cannot negate the theological implications of this incarnational moment. But this is of course a simple conjecture.

In the Christian mystical tradition, self-negation (*kenosis, apophasis*) symbolizes the death of Christ to the "old self," to the old Adam. This act of surrender prepares the way that led the mystic to self-affirmation (*pleroma, kataphasis*), or to the resurrection of the "new self" in Christ, in the new Adam. The symbol of the cross contains the mystery of Christ's death and

---

⁴⁰ John of the Cross, *The Collected Works*, 156; *Ascent* 2.2.1.

⁴¹ Ibid., 382; *Dark Night* 1.10.6.

⁴² Thomas Merton, *Seeds of Contemplation* (New York: A Dell Book, 1956), 40-41.

resurrection, but the symbol itself cannot be reduced to a single historical account of the crucifixion of Jesus of Nazareth.

If the latter theory is accepted, then, the mystery of the cross is reduced to one single, historical event, which undermines the universal appealing message of Christianity. In short, the symbol of the cross continues to be a constant source of inspiration for Christians and non-Christians alike because it captures the paradoxical nature of the Christian life, the death and resurrection of the self in Christ.

The human soul has an unrestricted desire to know the heart of Christ. By encountering God at the deepest center, the mystic receives infused knowledge (or what St. John of the Cross calls "*noticia amorosa*," a loving knowledge). This loving knowledge is "present in us in the form of that little point of nothingness and poverty in us which is the 'point' or virgin eye by which we know Him."[43]

St. John of the Cross also describes this state of pure nothingness with such expressions as "poverty of spirit," "dark night," "pure and naked faith," and so forth. The Spanish Carmelite, following these mystical expressions, writes the following:

> *Poor, abandoned, unsupported by any of the apprehensions of my soul ... left to darkness in pure faith, which is a dark night for these natural faculties, and with my will touched only by sorrows, afflictions, and longings of love of God, I went out from myself. That is, I departed from my low manner of understanding, and my feeble way of loving, and my poor and limited method of finding satisfaction in God ... This was great happiness a sheer grace for me, because through the annihilation and calming of my faculties, passions, appetites, and affections, by which my*

---

[43] Thomas Merton, *Conjectures of a Guilty Bystander* (New York: The Macmillan Company, 1967), 160.

> *experience and satisfaction in God were base, I went out from my human operation and way of acting to God's operation and way of acting.*[44]

For John, the dark night of the soul is the gift of pure contemplation. Merton, echoing John's description of the contemplative experience, says that "it is a deep resonance in the inmost center of our spirit in which our very life loses its separate voice and re-sounds with the majesty and the mercy of the Hidden and Living One."[45] Furthermore, "true contemplation means the complete destruction of all selfishness--the most pure poverty and cleanness of heart."[46]

Merton clearly understands that the symbol of the dark night could be interpreted in different ways. Merton states:

> *Just as Saint Gregory of Nyssa takes Moses through three stages in his ascent to God, so Saint John of the Cross divides his night into three [See 1 Ascent, 2,5. Peers tr., vol. 1, pp. 20-21, 66-69]:*

> *These three parts of the night are all one night; but like night itself, it has three parts. For the first part, which is that of the sense, is comparable to the beginning of night, the point at which things begin to fade from sight. And the second part, which is faith, is comparable to midnight, which is total darkness. And the third part is like the close of the night: which is God, the part which is near to the light of the day.*[47]

Ultimately, the dark night of St. John of the Cross ought to be described as the moment in which the human soul meets God at night when there is nothing to see, nothing to do, just rest in the divine night. The goal of the mystical union is achieved when the human soul is fully transformed in

---

[44] John of the Cross, *The Collected Works*, 400; *Dark Night* 2.4.1.2.

[45] Merton, *New Seeds of Contemplation*, 3. Merton, like St. John of the Cross, thinks of contemplation as "a pure and a virginal knowledge, poor in concepts, poorer still in reasoning, but able, by its very poverty and purity, to follow the Word 'wherever He may go'" (5).

[46] Ibid., 43.

[47] Thomas Merton, *The Ascent to Truth* (New York: A Harvest Book, 1981), 52. See John of the Cross, *The Collected Works*, 121.

God. This is the highest degree of perfection that one can reach in this life. The image of the activity of fire that has penetrated the wood, transformed it so inwardly that now "it is not merely united to this fire but produces within it a living flame."[48] The divine fire thereby does not consume the human soul for it "never kill[s] unless to give life, never wound unless to heal."[49]

For John, the transformative effect of the divine fire in the whole person "does not consume and destroy the soul in which it so burns. And it does not afflict it; rather, commensurate with the strength of the love, it divinizes and delights it, burning gently within it."[50] Merton puts it this way:

> *In the personal mystical experience of St. John of the Cross, God was known as "unknown," and the All was attained as "Nothingness" (Nada) ... Only those with a certain experience of the life of faith are able to apprehend these paradoxical statements without misinterpreting them as "atheism" or "pantheism."*[51]

For Merton, the SanJuanist apophatic mysticism of the dark night does not end in nihilism but, on the contrary, it ends with John's mystical theology of love. For John, the symbol of the dark night did not fall into a nihilistic existentialism but rather it was viewed as the highest expression of light, love, and truth. In the words of Merton:

The mystical night is not a mere night, absence of light. It is a night which is sanctified by the presence of an invisible light ... The night of faith has

---

[48] John of the Cross, *The Collected Works*, 639; *Living Flame of Love*, Prologue, 4.

[49] Ibid., 663; *Living Flame of Love* 2.16.

[50] Ibid., 658; *Living Flame of Love* 2.3.

[51] Thomas Merton, *Faith and Violence* (Notre Dame: University of Notre Dame Press, 1968), 270-271. In *Contemplation in a World of Action* (Boston: Mandala Books, 1980), Merton distinguishes the No-thingness of the mystic from that of the atheist. He declares:

> *As St. John of the Cross dared to say in mystical language, the term of the ascent of the mount of contemplation is "Nothing"— Y en el monte Nada. But the difference between the apophatic contemplative and the atheist may be purely negative, that of the contemplative is so to speak negatively positive (172-173).*

brought us into contact with the Object of all faith, not as an object but as a Person Who is the center and life of our own being, at once His own transcendent Self and the immanent source of our own identity and life.[52]

In short, St. John of the Cross builds his mysticism of wisdom based on the possibility that human beings can reach out to the divine in the here and now. By entering into the deepest states of contemplation and intuitive understanding, the mystic can feel the divine presence in all things. Everything seems to be charged with the divine life. Yet God remains a mystery, even to the mystic who has experienced the divine within. As Martin Buber poignantly observes:

> *He who enters on the absolute relation is concerned with nothing isolated any more, neither things nor beings, neither earth nor heaven; but everything is gathered up in the relation. For to step into pure relation is not disregard everything but to see everything in the Thou, not to renounce the world but to establish it on its true basis. To look away from the world, or to stare at it, does not help a man to reach God; but he who sees the world in Him stands in His presence ... Of course God is the "wholly Other"; but He is also the wholly Same, the wholly Present. Of course He is the Mysterium Tremendum that appears and overthrows; but He is also the mystery of the self-evident, nearer to me than my I.*[53]

---

[52] Thomas Merton, *The New Man* (New York: The Noonday Press, 1993), 247-248. Merton has previously asserted that "Our life of 'watching in the night,' of sharing in the resurrection of Christ . . . receives its most perfect liturgical expression in the Paschal Vigil" (238).

[53] Martin Buber, *I and Thou* (New York: Macmillan Publishing, 1987), 78-79. Buber's final words confirm God's mystery when he states: "The existence of mutuality between God and man cannot be proved, just as God's existence cannot be proved. Yet he who dares to speak of it, bears witness, and calls to witness him to whom he speaks . . ." (137).

5

THE MYSTICAL PATH OF DEVOTION

"[Y]a no guardo ganado,
ni ya tengo otro oficio,
que ya sólo en amar es mi ejercicio."
(poem from the *Spiritual Canticle*)

"I no longer tend the herd
nor have I any other trade
since now my sole occupation is to love."
(My own translation)

The "spirit" is the affective quality of sentient beings who are able to express "all forms of love, praise, thankfulness, adoration and celebration."[1] The metaphor of the "spirit" is suited to the mystical path of devotion found in the Hindu philosophy of *bhakti yoga*. The human soul attempts to become united with the divine through the path of the heart, which Robert Neville calls the path of the "saint." For Panikkar, the symbol that best represents the path of devotion is the element of fire. For St. John of the Cross the spiritual element of fire is without any doubt the most accessible element in his mystical theology, particularly discussed and explained in depth in the *Living Flame of Love*. According to the SanJuanist index, John used the word "fire" 310 times.[2]

---

[1] Panikkar, *Worship and Secular Man*, 86.

[2] Astigarraga, Borrell, and Martín, *Concordancias*, 865-869.

The word "devotion" often implies a pious way of living and acting in the world but most of the time is reduced to exterior practices (going to confession, participating in the Mass, and so forth). Although John lived a pious life, he was able to include in his devotional mystical theology any religious activity that leads the human soul to God.

John spent many hours praying and living his monastic rule to the fullest. He was sustained and nourished by the religious rituals and the discipline of the monastic tradition. He was famous for celebrating the Mass with great devotion and for having great liturgical festivities during Christmas or Easter. He used to dance with the child Jesus in Granada, as some witnesses (like María de la Cruz) declared in the depositions of Úbeda for his process of canonization and beatification.[3] He had great spiritual conversations with the novices and nuns. He served well as a spiritual director and confessor. It is also known that he was sent to preach in Duruelo, Mancera, and Beas, thus fulfilling his apostolic duties. All his action, thoughts, and devotions were dedicated to the glory of God.

Devout Christians believe that by imitating Christ one might reach salvation. St. John of the Cross lived his life following the example set by Jesus as the Christ. The Carmelite mystic desired to suffer and to be despised in this world, not because he was masochistic, but rather out of the religious conviction that his love for God, the universe, and all human beings was so great that any sense of pain will ultimately be redeemed by the power of love. Every single action offered to God in praise and adoration is, therefore, a labor of love.

John follows a long Christian devotional movement rooted in the path of love. There is no better testimony to John's devotion than his poetry. John bears witness in many of his commentaries on the *Living Flame of Love* what it is like to be united with God. However, John points out that "words

---

[3] Maria de la Cruz, "Proceso de Ubeda," in *Procesos de Beatificación y Canonización de San Juan de la Cruz*, Tomo V, eds. A. Fortes y F. J. Cuevas (Burgos: Editorial Monte Carmelo, 1994), 487.

are usually lacking"⁴ when the mystic tries to explain what is happening at the core of the human soul in his or her encounter with the divine. John further says: "one speaks badly of the intimate depths of the spirit if one does not do so with a deeply recollected soul."⁵

John puts experience first, before any attempt to describe how God's grace intervenes in the human soul. No one can truly explain this human-divine encounter without having been granted with the gift of divine grace. And even receiving "a heavenly gift from the Father of lights, from whom comes every excellent gift,"⁶ would not exhaust all the mysteries of the divine life.

John describes not only union of the soul in God but also transformation of the highest degree of perfection that one can reach in this life. He uses the image of the activity of fire that has penetrated the wood, transformed it so inwardly that now "it is not merely united to this fire but produces within it a living flame."⁷ The divine fire thereby does not consume the human soul, except in glory.

The transformative power exercised by the divine fire within the human soul shows how the person is not totally absorbed, extinguished, or annihilated in the divine. Rather, the soul is enriched, rekindled, delighted, enlarged, brightened, elevated to such a perfect love where the lover and the beloved are one, and the soul is not yet "in its deepest center, for it can go deeper in God."⁸ To put it differently, John declares that the effect of the divine fire in the person as a whole "does not consume and destroy the soul in which it so burns. And it does not afflict it; rather, commensurate

---

[4] John of the Cross, *The Collected Works*, 638; *Living Flame of Love*, Prologue, 1.

[5] Ibid.

[6] Jasper Hopkins, *Nicholas of Cusa On Learned Ignorance* (Minneapolis: The Arthur J. Banning Press, 1990), 158. See how John of the Cross uses the same terminology in the *Living Flame of Love* 1.15; 3.47 (John of the Cross, *The Collected Works*, 646; 692).

[7] John of the Cross, *The Collected Works*, 639; *Living Flame of Love*, Prologue, 4.

[8] Ibid., 645; *Living Flame of Love* 1.12.

with the strength of the love, it divinizes and delights it, burning gently within it."[9]

For John, what is destroyed is not the human self but rather "the imperfections of its bad habits."[10] Psychologically, what is destroyed is the person's egotistical desires, the attachments and bondage to things in themselves. Therefore, the lower self is not completely destroyed or annihilated because it forms an integral part of the whole person. What the religious person needs to do then is to train and transform these egotistical desires, these bad habits, and turn them into something good for the glory and honor of God so that he or she can participate more fully in the divine life.

John claims that humans can reach union with the divine, with "even the deep things of God [1 Cor. 2:10]," for "[t]he happy soul that by great fortune [God's grace] reaches this cautery knows all things, tastes all things, does all it wishes, and prospers."[11] This is why once the spiritual seeker has reached the summit, the contemplative no longer is attached to what others say about the divine life: for "the just man there is no law," because "he is a law unto himself."[12]

"Having made one with God," John says, "the soul is somehow God through participation. Although it is not God as perfectly as it will be in the next life, it is like the shadow of God."[13] The human soul "has become God through participation in God ... although the substance of this soul is not the substance of God."[14] Therefore, human souls by their efforts alone are incapable of reaching divine union. It is only by mutual consent that God and the human soul partake of this transformative union.

---

[9] Ibid., 658; *Living Flame of Love* 2.3.

[10] Ibid., 648; *Living Flame of Love* 1.19.

[11] Ibid., 659; *Living Flame of Love* 2.4.

[12] Ibid., 111; see the "Sketch of Mount Carmel" drawn by St. John of the Cross.

[13] Ibid., 706; *Living Flame of Love* 3.78.

[14] Ibid., 671; *Living Flame of Love* 2.34.

The spiritual marriage between the human and the divine, the lover and the beloved seems to happen in the eternal now which has "seas of loving fire within it, reaching to the heights and depths of the earthly and heavenly spheres, imbuing all with love. It seems to it that the entire universe is a sea of love in which it is engulfed, for conscious of the living point or center of love within itself, it is unable to catch sight of the boundaries of this love."[15] John's theology is heavenly marked by a cosmotheandric vision, using Raimundo Panikkar's words. Moreover, John writes: "Many saints have attained to this substantial touch during their lives on earth" for they can "have a certain savor of eternal life," because this touch truly "tastes of eternal life."[16] As a result, "the soul tastes here all the things of God."[17]

But is it really the goal of the Christian to spend eternity contemplating the vision of God alone? Or does the mystical experience leave in the human soul an unrestricted desire to share the fruits of contemplation with other human beings? The answer of a Christian mystic like John is clear; the command is to love one another as much as the Christian loves God. According to Friar Eliseo de los Mártires, John himself says:

Decía asimismo que el amor del bien de los prójimos nace de la vida espiritual y contemplativa, y que, como ésta se nos encarga por Regla, es visto encargado y mandarnos este bien y celo del aprovechamiento de nuestros prójimos; porque quiso la Regla hacer observantes de vida mixta y compuesta por incluir en sí abrazar las dos, activa y contemplativa. La cual escogió el Señor para sí por ser más perfecta.[18]

---

[15] Ibid., 661; *Living Flame of Love* 2.10.

[16] Ibid., 665; *Living Flame of Love* 2.21.

[17] Ibid.

[18] Crisógono de Jesús, Matías del Niño Jesús and Lucinio Ruano, *Vida y Obras de San Juan de la Cruz* (Madrid: Biblioteca de Autores Cristianos, 1978), 433; Advice, 9. The English translation reads:

John of the Cross understood the cosmic interdependence between the love of God with the love of neighbor and the world at large. He writes: "la compasión de los prójimos tanto más crece cuanto más el alma se junta con Dios por amor."[19] And Friar Eliseo de los Mártires also declares that "pareciéndoles poco ir solos al cielo, procuran con ansias y celestiales afectos y diligencias exquisitas llevar muchos al cielo consigo. Lo cual nace del grande amor que tienen a su Dios, y es propio fruto y efecto este de la perfecta oración y contemplación."[20]

John believes that all Christians are called to be contemplatives in action, although only a few reach "this high state of perfect union with God."[21] However, John also thinks that "the reason is not that God wishes only a few of these spirits to be so elevated; he would rather want all to be perfect, but he finds few vessels that will endure so lofty and sublime a work."[22] John might have thought that few people are really committed to walk through the narrow path in the ascent to God's summit (or to Mount Carmel, as his monastic tradition puts it in symbolic terms), for only a few can take the ordinary sufferings and sacrifices along the road.

St. Teresa of Ávila could not have said it better when she states:

> *The soul wants to flee people, and it has great envy of those who have lived in deserts. On the other hand, it would want to enter into the midst*

---

the love of neighbor is born in the spiritual and contemplative life . . . because the [Carmelite] precept wanted their members to follow the mixed life for it includes and embraces both the active and the contemplative. The Lord chose for himself the mixed life because it was the most perfect [my own translation].

[19] Ibid., 434; Advice, 10. The English text reads: "the compassion for our neighbor grows the more the soul is united with God by love" [my own translation].

[20] Ibid; Advice, 10. I translated this sentence into English as follows:

it seems to them little going to heaven alone, endeavouring with eagerness and celestial affection and exquisite diligence to take with them many souls to heaven. And this is born from the great love that these souls had for God, and [this] is [due to] the proper fruit and effect of the perfect prayer and contemplation.

[21] John of the Cross, *The Collected Works*, 667; *Living Flame of Love* 2.27.

[22] Ibid.

of the world to try to play a part in getting even one soul to praise God more. A woman in this stage of prayer is distressed by the natural hindrance there is to her entering the world, and she has great envy of those who have the freedom to cry out and spread the news abroad about who this great God of hosts.[23]

Teresa recognizes how difficult it is for the mystic to return to the world that was left behind as a spiritual practice (namely, *contemptus mundi* or *fuga mundi*) for the sake of communing with God alone. Subsequently, the genuine mystic turns into a prophet by responding with great courage and freedom to the "news abroad about who this great God of hosts is."[24]

Teresa's incarnational spirituality demands a prophetic response from the person who has been blessed by God's grace. Her spiritual pragmatism led to action by making every possible effort to reach out to those who were in spiritual and material need. For Teresa, the purpose of the spiritual marriage was "always of good works, good works."[25]

There have been a few good comparative studies focusing on the relationship between Teresa and John, but it would be important in this study to compare their shared symbol of the dark night. As Fülöp-Miller points out:

Teresa and John were of different worldly lineage, of different sex and of different age; yet they were both of the same spiritual lineage, of the same spiritual sex and had the same spiritual maturity. They both were mystics, poets, and saints. What distinguished them outwardly, was eliminated by an inner identity of purpose and ideal. Their work was enlivened by the same spirit, the same holiness. It was destined to be a unique kind of work, for the quietude of their hearts and the mysticism

---

[23] Teresa of Avila, *The Collected Works*, 392; *Interior Castle* 6.6.3.

[24] Ibid.

[25] Ibid., 446; *Interior Castle* 7.4.6.

of their minds united these two visionaries in practical activity and made of stillness and vision an earthly reality.[26]

Spiritually, it seems like both Teresa and John experienced union with God in this life. Most scholars agree, after having read their mystical writings and the witnesses' reports, that both experienced union with the divine. They had several mystical experiences. In 1554, Teresa at the age of forty would undergo her first personal encounter with Christ; however, at this time she was kneeling at an image of the crucified Christ recently placed in a corridor of the Incarnation.

This sudden religious conversion was seen by some Teresian scholars as fruit of her dedicated life to God. Teresa claimed she experienced raptures, moments when she was lifted up out of herself and turned into God's presence. She felt the Lord's presence accompanying her everywhere. Likewise, John claimed to have experienced God at the deepest center of his soul. His brother Francisco reported that John told him about his mystical vision of Christ in Segovia. Perhaps the best testimony lies in his mystical poetry and theological commentaries. John writes in the Prologue of the *Ascent of Mount Carmel*:

> *A deeper enlightenment and wider experience than mine is necessary to explain the dark night through which a soul journeys toward that divine light of perfect union with God that is achieved, insofar as possible in this life, through love. The darkness and trials, spiritual and temporal, that fortunate souls ordinarily undergo on their way to the high state of perfection are so numerous and profound that human science cannot understand them adequately. Nor does experience of them equip one to explain them. Only those who suffer them will know what this experience is like, but they won't be able to describe it.*[27]

---

[26] Fülöp-Miller, *The Saints that Moved the World*, 454.

[27] John of the Cross, *The Collected Works*, 114-115; *Ascent*, Prologue, 1.

In that passage, John's treatment of suffering is not so much a matter of being persecuted or tormented by his enemies, but rather the highest degree of contemplation that one can experience in this life. The mystic suffers in his or her life the divine touch of love which transforms and elevates those who are blessed by the divine hand. John also writes in the Prologue of the *Spiritual Canticle*:

> *These stanzas, Reverend Mother [Ana de Jesús (Lobera)], were obviously composed with a certain burning love of God ... It would be foolish to think that expressions of love arising from mystical understanding, like these stanzas, are fully explainable ... Who can describe in writing the understanding he gives to loving souls in whom he dwells? And who can express with words the experience he imparts to them? Who, finally, can explain the desires he gives them? Certainly, no one can! Not even they who receive these communications ... Since these stanzas, then, were composed in a love flowing from abundant mystical understanding, I cannot explain them adequately, nor is it my intention to do so ... I believe such an explanation will be more suitable. It is better to explain the utterances of love in their broadest sense so that each one may derive profit from them according to the mode and capacity of one's own spirit, rather than narrow them down to a meaning unadaptable to every palate.*[28]

John clearly suggested that even the mystic cannot fully describe what God is since God is not an object. Perhaps this idea might explain why John chose the symbol of the dark night. Mystical theologians accept the impossibility of communicating the received divine revelations unless the message is conveyed through symbols and signs. And poetry is perhaps the best medium that John knew of explaining the unexplainable. John also said that each one is free to interpret the divine utterances in his mystical poetry according to the degree of initiation into the spiritual life. John rejected, therefore, any attempt to "narrow down" the meaning of his

---

[28] Ibid., 469-470; *Spiritual Canticle*, Prologue, 1-2.

poetry. Yet he provided some hints on how to interpret his mystical experiences. He states:

> *And that my explanations--which I desire to submit to anyone with better judgment than mine and entirely to Holy Mother the Church-- may be worthy of belief, I do not intend to affirm anything of myself or trust in any of my own experiences or in those of other spiritual persons whom I have known or heard of. Although I plan to make use of these experiences, I want to explain and confirm at least the more difficult matters through passages from Sacred Scripture.*[29]

John submitted his theological commentaries to the authority of the Roman Catholic Church, knowing that in his time Lutherans and New Christians were persecuted by the Inquisition, because they freely interpreted biblical passages (Luis de León), or they communicated certain thoughts that sounded unorthodox (Miguel de Molinos). However, John clearly stated that he would make use of his experiences to explain difficult spiritual matters from the Bible.

Teresa, like John, viewed the biblical story of Martha and Mary as the sistole and diastole of the Christian spiritual life. Genuine contemplation always leads to good deeds. The unselfish service that these two Carmelite contemplatives offered to the world remind us of the labor of love and the high price they paid embarking in their Discalced Carmelite reform.

Carmelite spirituality does not seek solitude and silence as ends in themselves. But, in reality, what the Carmelite prophetic mystical tradition sought from its beginning was not solitude but solidarity. By displaying acts of compassion and empathy towards others, the monk or the nun fulfills his or her religious vocation in the world.

To be a Carmelite is to embody the Carmelite ideal. Again, the etymological meaning of the Hebrew word "Carmel" (רְמִלַּכ) is often translated as God's paradise or garden. Carmelites are called to build the kingdom of

---

[29] Ibid., 471; *Spiritual Canticle*, Prologue, 4.

God on earth. They make it possible for the ideal to become a reality. For them, the dichotomy presented to us between the life of contemplation and the life of action, between the mystical life and the prophetic life, is an artificial creation that impedes human beings from reaching their full potential, which has as it highest goal to love God, humanity, and creation. Thomas Merton puts it well when he says:

> *There is no contradiction between action and contemplation when Christian apostolic activity is raised to the level of pure charity. On that level, action and contemplation are fused into one entity by the love of God and our brother in Christ. But the trouble is that if prayer is not itself deep, powerful and pure and filled at all times with the spirit of contemplation, Christian action can never really reach this high level ... Without them our apostolate is more for our own glory than for the glory of God.*[30]

The goal of the Christian mystic is to become God by participation so that the contemplative can share the fruits of his or her mystical vision with others by becoming a messenger of God on earth. St. John of the Cross clearly granted the possibility that some blessed souls become God by participation calling this transformative unitive experience of the human soul in God, "*a lo divino.*" Mystical theologians called this process of divinization, *theosis,* or pleromatization. Therefore, one might conclude that John seems to be closer to the Eastern (Orthodox) Church in his elaborated theology of partakers of the divine glory in God. Nonetheless, John's panentheistic mystical theology is perhaps rooted in the Pauline recapitulation of all things in Christ. As Manuela Dunn Mascetti notes:

> *It is easy to forget that the Orthodox doctrine of deification was biblically based. In the famous saying of Peter, Christ saved us so that "we may become partakers of the divine nature" (2 Peter 1:4). Orthodox theo-*

---

[30] Merton, *Contemplative Prayer*, 115.

logians leaned on this and other passages in creating this teaching. (See especially John 17:22-3 and 2 Corinthians 8:9).[31]

Now, the fully integrated and matured Christian fully abides and fully lives in the glory of God forever. Merton argues that

> [t]o admit, with St. John of the Cross, that we encounter God in the "inmost center" (or "ground") of our own being is not to deny His personality but to affirm it more forcefully than ever, for He is also, precisely, the cause of our own personality and it is in response to His love that our freedom truly develops to personal maturity.[32]

John's theology of love is trinitarian in its approach because the human soul partakes of the divine life by participating, here and now, in God's glory, in eternal life, "since it raises them up to the activity of God in God."[33] God made the soul experience the living God of the Bible so that the human soul can "taste the living God--that is, God's life, eternal life."[34]

As John points out: "The Blessed Trinity inhabits the soul by divinely illumining its intellect with the wisdom of the Son, delighting its will in the Holy Spirit, and absorbing it powerfully and mightily in the unfathomed embrace of the Father's sweetness."[35] Or as John puts it: "The cautery is the Holy Spirit, the hand is the Father, and the touch is the Son."[36]

---

[31] Mascetti, *Christian Mysticism*, 99.

[32] Merton, *Faith and Violence*, 270-271. Consequently, the divinization process of the human soul does not imply in the Christian mystical tradition a loss of human personality. Rather, it is in this union that the human soul gained her character, her true identity, by becoming God by participation. Merton writes: "This perfect union is not a fusion of natures but a unity of love and of experience. The distinction between the soul and God is no longer experienced as a separation into subject and object when the soul is united to God" (*Thomas Merton Reader*, 515).

[33] John of the Cross, *The Collected Works*, 642; *Living Flame of Love* 1.4.

[34] Ibid., 643; *Living Flame of Love* 1.6.

[35] Ibid., 646; *Living Flame of Love* 1.15.

[36] Ibid., 658; *Living Flame of Love* 2.1.

John's mystical path of devotion is undoubtedly linked to the path of love. The Carmelite mystics believe that there is no higher religion than love. And it is the Christian mystics who eventually affirm that there is no higher theological virtue than love.

6

THE SANJUANIST LEGACY FOR TODAY'S WORLD

John primarily is known today as a poet, mystic, and theologian, even though those roles are but a few of his most important contributions. In addition, he was for a long time depicted as an abstruse thinker, lacking originality and intellectual vigor. Thus, John's intellectual capacities were almost forgotten or overlooked for several centuries.

In the twentieth century, John started to gain recognition as a poet and artist. Poets from all over the world, including Federico García Lorca and Pablo Neruda, have paid their homage to John on numerous occasions. In 1952, the Spanish ministry of education named John the patron of the Spanish poets. Furthermore, eco-theologians find John's poetry a major source of inspiration. John clearly understood the relationships between God, humanity, and the world. For Keith J. Egan,

The poetry of John of the Cross reveals his profound affection and appreciation for the beauty of nature. His poetry is a veritable thesaurus of nature's images, many of which come from the lush imagery in the Song of Songs or from his keen appreciation of creation. For John, faith in Christ is greeted as "¡Oh cristalina fuente, O spring-like crystal!"[1]

---

[1] Keith Egan, "Dark Night," in *Carmel and Contemplation*, 244-245.

Additionally, John the artist gained the status of celebrity thanks to Salvador Dalí. The world-renowned Spanish painter gave John credit for his painting of the resurrected Christ. which is normally exhibited in the Kelvingrove Art Gallery and Museum in Glasgow, Scotland. Dalí was truly inspired by John's drawing of Christ after Fr. Crisógono took him to see it in Ávila. Both artists tried to capture in their drawings the mystery of Christ.

Moreover, musicians have used John's poems and lyrics as texts for musical setting and inspiration. It is not surprising at all to find among these song-writers names like Amancio Prada or Leonard Bernstein. Even flamenco singers and guitarists, like Enrique Morente, Carmen Linares, or Paco Cortés, have translated John's lyrical poems into music. Having John's original intention in mind, these artists would recite his poems aloud. Without doubt, John's brother Francisco, who was popular in small Spanish towns for his musical talent as a singer, exercised a great influence on John's folkloric culture. Spanish filmmaker Carlos Saura has also told the story of St. John of the Cross's imprisonment in Toledo in his film *La Noche Oscura*.

The following list summarizes John's artistic accomplishments according to Keith Egan:

> *John was a many-sided artist. Salvador Dali took inspiration from John's sketch of Christ Crucified, and critics have admired this sketch for its artistic originality. John also had the eye of an architect. He designed and built the aqueduct and cloister at Granada, and he worked with the young artist who sculpted and painted at the Carmelite foundation at Baeza. John also liked to carve crucifixes and other images. In his writings, he frequently turned to imagery taken from painting and carving, and John of the Cross loved music and singing. His sensitivity to the beauty of music is apparent in his commentary on the celebrated phrase "silent music [.]"*[2]

---

[2] Ibid., 244.

A major problem raised by commentators is the propensity in SanJuanist studies to separate John's sublime mystical poetry from his mystical theology. These two major schools of thought have different interests and methodologies in approaching the saint's mystical teachings. On the one hand, there are commentators, mainly philosophers and theologians, who see poetry as irrelevant for understanding the mystical experience. On the other hand, there are some commentators, especially literary critics, who think that theological understanding is unnecessary since John's poetry is closer in meaning to his mystical experience.

In fairness to the spirit of the Carmelite saint, it has been the purpose of this study to carefully analyze John's writings in reference to his secondary sources by utilizing all the available data at the present time. I would suggest that poetry and theology must be brought together for a full understanding of John's integral Christian humanism. John's poetry is intuitive, direct, and experiential, whereas his theology is analytical, reflective, and rational. One complements the other. As Willis Barnstone puts it:

> *San Juan was a mystical poet because in a formal sense his poems were written, he himself states, as a result of mystical knowledge, and in his commentaries, he endeavors to explain the poems, in great detail, as steps toward the mystical union. The question of whether mysticism is a valid religious experience or a form of hysteria, hallucination, psychedelic substitute, or sublimated sexual ectsasy, or even whether the poems themselves convey the mystical experience, is secondary and not the issue. The point I wish to make clear is that the appellation mystical poet, Doctor Místico as he was called, is correct in that San Juan was himself a mystic and the origin of his poems lies in the mystical experience.*[3]

St. John of the Cross the mystical poet is often depicted in his ecstatic moments of union with God. The Carmelite mystic seems oblivious to the world. The poet's only concern is to be alone with God. As some literary critics note, "San Juan de la Cruz (1542-1591) was the last great figure of

---

[3] Barnstone, *The Poems of Saint John of the Cross*, 24-25.

Mysticism in Spain and represents its highest flights. His poetry is the most intense and metaphysical, the most abstract and pure, of all mystic poets."[4]

But is it so? Didn't John dedicate many of his poems and commentaries to nuns and lay people, in an effort to confront their inner and outer struggles on a daily basis? Wasn't he concerned about the special relationship between God, the world, and human beings? Why then is John's personality characterized as "metaphysical" or fond of abstractions?

It is not entirely surprising at all to find out that John never had the popular appeal of other saints. Many witnesses have reported that John underwent deep states of absorption in God; they report especially seeing him unceasingly meditating with God for hours. According to Thomas Dubay,

> *Sheer sanctity was his [John] paramount trait. This man was on fire, utterly absorbed in God. He experienced ecstatic prayer even though he said almost nothing about the subject (because "Madre Teresa" had already so well said all that needed to be said about it), and he reached the transforming union while still a young man. The saint was capable of an absorption during meals such that he could not recall what he had eaten--much like St. Thomas Aquinas, who provided his own anesthetic for bleeding by the simple procedure of going into contemplative prayer.*[5]

As a mystic, John's popularity did not cross the Spanish borders until he was beatified, canonized, and proclaimed a Doctor of the Catholic Church. Although the Carmelite saint was not widely recognized outside Spain until recent times, most of his contemporaries knew him as a holy man, even before he was proclaimed a saint.

---

[4] Richard E. Chandler and Kessel Schwartz, *A New History of Spanish Literature* (Baton Rouge, Lousiana: Louisiana State University Press, 1991), 221.

[5] Thomas Dubay, *Fire Within*: *St. Teresa of Avila, St. John of the Cross, and the Gospel--on Prayer* (San Francisco: Ignatius Press, 1989), 35.

Miguel de Cervantes y Saavedra probably alluded to John's dead body in *Don Quixote* 1.19. In a chapter entitled, "Of the shrewd things that Sancho Panza said to his master and the adventure that happened to him in connection with a dead body, along with other famous events," Cervantes tells a story about a religious friar whose dead corpse has been secretly moved from Baeza, a town near Úbeda, to Segovia. Literary critics and theologians (Navarrete, Muñoz Iglesias) have found this event closely associated with the historical move of John's body from Úbeda to Segovia in 1593. As Henry E. Watts points out in one of the many critical editions of *Don Quixote*:

> *Navarrete, in his Life of Cervantes, tells a curious story, which he believes to be the original of this adventure. In 1591, a certain holy monk, San Juan de la Cruz, died in his convent at Ubeda, which is near Baeza, of a pestilent fever – calenturas pestilentes – whose body, after being buried nine months, was removed at night in great secrecy to another convent at Segovia, many strange signs and omens attending the translation. The saint was found fresh and uncorrupted, distilling sweet odours. On the road a man appeared suddenly on top of a high hill, and called out in a loud voice, "Whither are ye taking the saint's body? Leave it where it was." Before it reached Segovia, the corpse-bearers testified to seeing, during its transit, many shining lights round about the chest which contained the venerable relic.*
>
> *The affair ended in a suit by the city of Ubeda against the city of Segovia, heard before Pope Clement VIII, who ordered the restitution of the holy remains to their original tomb. Ultimately, so great was the reluctance of the Segovians to part with the sacred corpse, a compromise was made with the people of Ubeda, the saint's body being divided between the two cities. Cervantes was in the province of Granada about the date of this affair, which made much noise at the time, and it may be that it gave him a hint for Don Quixote's adventure, and also an occasion, such as he rarely misses, of having a sly hit at the clericals.*[6]

---

[6] Henry E. Watts, ed. *Don Quixote* (London: Bernard Quaritch, 1888), 250-251.

According to the Spanish theologian, Salvador Muñoz Iglesias, the adventures or misadventures of Cervantes' story in chapter nineteen clearly alluded to the translation of John's dead body from Úbeda to Segovia. However, Cervantes's originality did not lie so much in the power of retelling John's historical events. Rather, the celebrated Spanish writer deliberately distorted these historical events so that the story would fit into his narrative scheme.[7] In so doing, Cervantes achieved a highly artistic expression in the world of literature by virtue of deforming reality, which parallels the mannerist painting techniques used by the Greek-Spanish painter, El Greco.

John is recognized today as one of the most important mystics partly as a result of Pius XI declaring him the Mystical Doctor of the Roman Catholic Church. Numerous studies on John's mysticism, from Miguel Asín Palacios to William Johnston, have been published since then. However, John is still today characterized by SanJuanist commentators as an austere ascetic mystic who loved the detachment of *la nada*. Yet John is also the writer of the *Living Flame of Love*.

As a philosopher and theologian, John was underrated for many centuries. It was the works of twentieth century French philosophers like Jean Baruzi, Henri Bergson, and Jacques Maritain that resurrected John by placing him on top of the list of philosophers and mystical theologians of all times. Philosophers tend to be suspicious of mystical thinkers either because they subordinate reason to faith or simply because they want to transcend and move beyond the realm of reason altogether. Ironically, theologians are also very threatened by mystics because their dogmas and doctrines sometimes are not in tune with the language of the mystics.

St. John of the Cross develops a mystical theology of "final integration" by seeing the sacramental life as the body of religion in a twofold way which can be best expressed through the inner life of the liturgy during Mass, and through the outer life of carrying out the Christian message to the

---

[7] Salvador Muñoz Iglesias, *Lo Religioso en el Quijote* (Toledo: Estudio teológico de S. Ildefonso, 1989), 101.

world by engaging with the social and apostolic issues of one's time; it also consists of seeing the theological life as the head of religion, and the mystical life as the heart and dynamo of religion. These three aspects of religion – the sacramental, the theological, and the mystical – are well integrated in the life events and thoughts of St. John of the Cross.

A mystical theology of "final integration" (a coined term that I borrow from Reza Arasteh), is a holistic model which attempts to overcome the apparent dualism that exists between contemplation and action, spirit and body, the sacred and the secular. In the words of Thomas Merton:

> *The ideal of the contemplative life is not, however, the exclusion of all work. On the contrary, total inactivity would stultify the interior life just as much as too much activity. The true contemplative is one who has discovered the art of finding leisure even in the midst of his work, by working with such a spirit of detachment and recollection that even his work is a prayer.*[8]

The SanJuanist mystical theology provides concrete and practical guidelines in addressing the physical, mental, and spiritual needs of the whole person. St. John of the Cross was a mystic of action who responded prophetically to the social and religious issues of his time. By being firmly rooted in the eremitical-prophetic Carmelite tradition, John was able to reach out to those in need by virtue of his apostolic ministry. In monitoring the progress made by friars and nuns in their respective ministries, John avoided the sorts of religious trapping of a contemplative Docetism which was prevalent in some religious circles of his time, especially in monastic communities. The Carmelite mystic recognized his social and religious responsibility to be morally engaged in his time. And because John had the courage to follow God's calling, he suffered persecution.

The prophetic mysticism of St. John of the Cross is sharply at odds with the old Carmelite picture of a contemplative who completely withdrew

---

[8] Thomas Merton, *Spiritual Direction & Meditation* (Collegeville, Minnesota: The Liturgical Press, 1960), 86.

from society in search of God. John's mysticism does not reject the human condition in order to seek one's own individual salvation without manifesting any concern for the rest of humanity and all other creatures. Nor is his mysticism a matter of praying all day inside a monastic community for the sake of saving his soul. As Bernard McGuinn notes:

> *A large part of the secret of the Carmelite contribution seems to have been found in the ongoing tension between the desire for solitude--that is, withdrawal into the desert, especially the desert of the heart--and the need to be actively engaged in the work of spreading God's love in the world ... In an activist age and in a culture that tends to prize action above contemplation, this part of the Carmelite heritage is important both for the Carmelites themselves and for the witness they give to the rest of us.*[9]

It is important to understand John's writings in the historical context of sixteenth-century Spain. To illustrate this point: Merton rightly attributed the extremist austerity to John's age in general and to the new ideas implemented by Doria as the general *definitor* of the Discalced Carmelite order. He writes:

> *In the sixteenth century, within the Discalced Reform, there was also an extreme wing which sought solitude along with austerity and centralization: and this was the faction of Doria and the Friars of Pastrana, who eventually persecuted St. John of the Cross, and hounded him to his death. The curious thing is that St. John of the Cross, the defender of the pure Carmelite ideal of mystical contemplation, was himself not an extremist in favor of pure solitude, nor did he advocate extreme austerity, but took the middle way, favoring the combination of solitude and contemplation with preaching and the direction of souls.*[10]

---

[9] Bernard McGinn, "The Role of the Carmelites in the History of Western Mysticism," in *Carmel and Contemplation*, 47.

[10] Thomas Merton, *Disputed Questions* (New York: Mentor-Omega Book), 179-180.

According to Merton, John never approved extreme ascetic practices within the Carmelite reform, although some ascetic measures (that is, fasting, meditation, penance, mortification, prayer, and the like) must be exercised to a certain degree to prepare the soul for union with God. For John, asceticism is not an end in itself. The purpose of performing ascetic practices is to purify the senses and the spirit so that union with God can occur. Asceticism and mysticism go hand in hand. They need each other. I think that Allison Peers correctly understands the problem when he says:

> [N]or, in spite of his own ascetic life, does he forget the harmful possibilities of over-austerity. Even mortifications may be a hindrance to devotion. "Bodily penance, without obedience, is a most imperfect thing, for beginners are moved to it solely by the pleasure and delight which it brings them; and, therein following their own will, they grow rather in vice than in virtue."[11]

Additionally, E. W. Trueman Dicken says of John and Teresa that

> [t]he excesses of austerity and harsh discipline perpetrated by certain members of the Reform seemed to them quite fanatical. St Teresa herself abhorred this indiscreet zeal, as did St John of the Cross, but the Calced Carmelites dreaded it as a fire which might consume them all. The nuns at Paterna, a convent of the Mitigation which went over in toto to the Reform, had some most unhappy experiences, and certain of the Discalced showed every sign of attempting to reform the entire Order, including houses whose members were frankly quite incapable of living according to the Primitive Rule.[12]

An interpretation of the life and the mystical doctrine of St. John of the Cross from an extremist asceticism which reflects a dualistic worldview (God vs. the world, grace vs. nature, spirit vs. flesh), or from a supernaturalist perspective which portrays John devoid of his humanity, no longer represents an accurate picture of the Carmelite saint. As Paul J. Bernadicou

---

[11] E. Allison Peers, *Studies of the Spanish Mystics* (London: The Sheldon Press, 1927), 254.

[12] Dicken, *The Crucible of Love*, 20-21.

observes: "Though his [John's] age put much emphasis on penitential austerities as preliminary requisites, his path stayed grounded in the faith, hope, and love that marked one as an authentic follower of Jesus in the gospel tradition."[13]

A major problem is introduced in SanJuanist studies when John's *contemptus mundi* is interpreted as a total withdrawal from the world, meaning that the world and God are antithetical. But was John a dualist? For René Fülöp-Miller, John's withdrawal was not seen as escapism but rather he was well-grounded in the apostolic ministry of the Teresian reform. He states:

> *He [John] had turned his back on the world and sought the safety of a God-pleasing life in a Carmelite monastery. But in the worldly bustle of contemporary monasticism he had not found the answer to his quest and was convinced that salvation could only be attained in the spirit of Teresa's reform.*[14]

How did St. John of the Cross view the complex relationship between God, the world, and the human soul? In spite of being portrayed as a dualistic thinker, John was able to develop a mystical theology based on mutual love and reciprocity where God is constantly reaching out and seeking to become one with the human soul and the world at large. According to Willis Barnstone, John "withdrew from the world to be closer to his God, yet nature and human love are the key to his poetry."[15] Additionally, John Welch denies that John's spirituality scorns this world. He writes:

> *Through self-knowledge and through engagement with this world we come to know the God who is present in this creation. The experience of God is an experience of the transcendent dimension present in ordinary human experience. An interpretation of John's spirituality which would find no place for this world and its wonders would be a misreading. John*

---

[13] Paul J. Bernadicou, "Contemporary Guides to John of the Cross," *Spiritual Life* 44:1 (1998): 4-5.

[14] Fülöp-Miller, *The Saints that Moved the World*, 454.

[15] Barnstone, *The Poems of Saint John of the Cross*, 10.

appreciated settings such as the location of the Carmelite house on the hill of the Alhambra overlooking Granada, and the house in Segovia with its view of a wide sky, hills, and the striking Alcazar. Reports tell of John spending long hours outside at night letting nature speak of God.[16]

Philosophically, David B. Perrin, paraphrasing Georges Morel, suggests that "[t]he self-realization of the human person is founded in the movement of Self-revelation of the Absolute through love in the world. Using this basis, Morel shows the philosophical importance, as well as the contemporary importance, of SanJuanist mysticism."[17] Theologically, John places the golden rule and his theology of love at the heart of his faith: "You shall love the Lord your God with your whole heart, your whole soul, and with all your mind ... You shall love your neighbor as yourself" (Mt 22:37-39). In a nutshell, John summarizes his mystical theology by declaring that "the entire universe is a sea of love."[18]

John, like other Christian mystics (Eckhart and Boëhme, to name two), has been criticized for being a pantheist. But was John really a pantheist or rather a panentheist? Clearly John was a panentheist. He leaves room for divine transcendence, which most pantheist thinkers deny altogether, but he also stresses divine immanence following the Christian belief that God is constantly participating in history and in nature. The Christian God not only creates the universe but also is present to it by virtue of sharing one of the main divine attributes, namely being omnipresent.

Thus, John is without any doubt a panentheist because he holds the view that God is in all things and all things are in God in the same manner that St. Paul said God was, is, and shall be "all in all" (1 Cor. 15:28). John also claims that God, the world, and the human souls are not the same,

---

[16] John Welch, *An Introduction to John of the Cross: When Gods Die* (New York: Paulist Press, 1990), 182.

[17] David B. Perrin, "Foundations for a Hermeneutical Interpretation of the *Cántico Espiritual* of Juan de la Cruz," *Science et Esprit* 48:1 (1996): 76.

[18] John of the Cross, *The Collected Works*, 661; *Living Flame of Love* 2.10.

although they share oneness with one another. The world and the human soul share divinity by participation in the Godhead, not by essence.

As a Christian, John is well aware of the special relationship that exists between God and the world because his mystical theology is incarnational. John firmly believes that God is constantly participating in history, in creation. As a result of that conviction, John sees the universe as the unfolding of God's loving presence throughout time. For John, as for Plato, time is "the moving image of eternity." There is no radical dualism in John's mysticism. The passage of time is a sign of God's participation in history by virtue of sharing one of "His" divine attributes with the other monotheistic religious faiths, namely being omnipresent.

Camille Campbell, as a follower of the creation spirituality movement in the United States. and José Vicente Rodríguez, in Spain, have noticed the many references that John dedicated in his poems and commentaries to creation.[19] Clearly John includes in his writings many ecological themes that he experienced first-hand during his multiple walks and trips through the Iberian Peninsula. For instance, the green valleys of Segovia, the flat lands of Castile, the desert areas of la Peñuela, all of them became part of John's spiritual geography.

John's cosmological views are shaped by his personal reflections on the universe, being described as "a sea of love," and by the Pauline universal message that God shall be "all in all" (1 Cor. 15:28). As a student in Salamanca, John was also introduced to the new scientific theories and models, especially those interpreted and taught by a Copernican professor of the University of Salamanca named Hernando de Aguilera. According to Kieran Kavanaugh,

> *It seems John accepted the Copernican theory [See the Living Flame of Love 4.4]. In the first edition of his works (1618), the editor changed the*

---

[19] Rodríguez, José Vicente. *Florecillas de San Juan de la Cruz: La hondura de lo humano* (Madrid: Ediciones Paulinas, 1990) 192-215.

> text to read *"if the earth were to move, all natural things in it would move."* The University of Salamanca, where John studied, was the first to accept and teach the Copernican system. By the time the first edition appeared, Copernicus' work was on the Index of Forbidden Books.[20]

In the words of Jose Luis Sánchez Lora, a careful reading of John's writings might suggest a Copernican influence in his mystical theology. For instance, Sánchez Lora compares the following two passages (one from Copernicus, the other from St. John of the Cross):

Para Copérnico el movimiento circular "siempre gira regularmente, pues tiene una causa constante" ... Y para San Juan de la Cruz: "Estos visos de gloria que se dan en el alma son estables, perfectos y continuos" ... "y parece moverse él en ellas y ellas en él con movimiento continuo. Y por eso le parece al alma que él se movió, y recordó, siendo ella la movida y la recordada."[21]

From this study one thing becomes clear. St. John of the Cross was ahead of his time because he had the intellectual capacity to link the scientific, the literary, and the theological sources of his day. One could say, then, that John's creative synthesis is a reflection of the new intellectual movements that originated in sixteenth-century Europe. It has been suggested from previous sources that John belonged to the Renaissance age, although he was still living under the control of a medieval Church. In actuality, John played an important role as a pioneer thinker in the Christian humanist movement of the Iberian Peninsula.

---

[20] Ibid., 709.

[21] Jose Luis Sánchez Lora, *San Juan de la Cruz en la Revolución Copernicana* (Madrid: Editorial de Espiritualidad, 1992), 58. The English translations of the two selected passages are the following:

> For Copernicus the circular movement *"always moves continuously, because it has a constant cause"* [My own translation]. *"These glimpses of glory given to the soul are stable, perfect, and continuous. . .,"* "and God seemingly moved within them and they in Him with continuous movement. And because of that it will seem to the soul that God moved, and remembered, being the soul the one who was moved and remembered" [My own translation].

As a bridge builder, John understood quite well the relationship between primitive and medieval Christianity, especially in the context of monasticism. Yet John was a man of the Renaissance Age by having one foot at the gates of modernity and another foot anchored in the primitive Church. By incorporating new theories and ideas unheard of in his own time, John undisputedly contributed to the spiritual progress of sixteenth century Europe.

Proof of that is the fact that centuries later he was admired by people from all corners of the world, even in Asia where Eastern religious leaders have suggested that John was a sort of spiritual guru. As Swami Siddheswarananda says, "Among the Christian mystics, to whom in one way or another we can apply the term Yogi, St. John of the Cross can be called the yogi *par excellence*, because in him alone do we find all the elements of different yogas harmonised by the supremacy of Christian faith."[22]

Another scholar who has attempted to do a comparative study between the Bhagavad Gita and St. John of the Cross is Rudolf V. D'Souza. Unfortunately, both authors associate *karma yoga* with the purgative way and ignore altogether the mystical path of action and selfless service in the Spanish Carmelite saint.[23]

The contemplative John was also ahead of his time when he rightly saw the urgent necessity of courageously confronting the problems that were affecting the fragile thread of the Iberian family. John advocated for a non-violent way to shed light on the injustices committed in his own time, following the Christian principles of the Gospels. For John, the true contemplative was not only the blessed soul who achieves union with God in this

---

[22] Siddheswarananda, Swami. *Hindu Thought and Carmelite Mysticism*. Translated by William Buchanan (Delhi: Motilal Banarsidass Publishers, 1998) 150.

[23] Rudolf V. D'Souza, *The BhagavadGita and St. John of the Cross: A Comparative Study of the Dynamism of Spiritual Growth in the Process of God-Realisation* (Roma: Editrice Pontificia Universita Gregoriana, 1996) 378-393.

life but also one who works for peace and unity in the world. "The finally integrated man is a peacemaker,"[24] as Thomas Merton notes.

John was able to create in the midst of a harsh environment of hatred and resentment a non-violent, loving response to those who characterized themselves as his enemies. In his famous twenty-sixth letter addressed to Mother María de la Encarnación, John writes: "Y adonde no hay amor, ponga amor, y sacará amor.[25]

John exposed in public the systematic expressions of sin that were part of the social and the religious establishment of his time. He chose writing, preaching, confession, and spiritual direction as the prophetic mediums for speaking out against such injustices as intolerance, hunger, illiteracy, or mistreatment of women.

Another major contribution of John's mysticism is his study of divine wisdom as the feminine image of God. There are countless passages in John's writings where the Carmelite refers to God as *hagia sophia* following the Greek tradition, *chokmah* in the Jewish tradition, and *sapientia* in the Latin tradition. For instance, John attributes the title of divine wisdom to the "Son of God."[26] In another passage, John clearly identifies wisdom as the feminine divine image of the Godhead by saying:

> *Divine Wisdom speaks, here, to all those who are attached to the things of the world. She calls them little ones because they become as little as the things they love. She tells them, accordingly, to be cunning and careful, that she is dealing with great things, not small things, as they are; and that the riches and glory they love are with her and in her, not where they think; and that lofty riches and justice are present in her.*

---

[24] Thomas Merton, *Contemplation in a World of Action* (London: Unwin Paperbacks, 1980), 212.

[25] Eulogio Pacho, ed. *S. Juan de la Cruz. Obras Completas* (Burgos: Monte Carmelo, 1993), 1315. For the English translation, see John of the Cross, *The Collected Works*, 760. "And where there is no love, put love, and you will draw love."

[26] John of the Cross, *The Collected Works*, 199; *Ascent* 2.15.4. In the *Spiritual Canticle* 3.3, John defines divine wisdom as "the Son of God, her Spouse."

> *Although in their opinion the things of the world are riches, she tells them to bear in mind that her riches are more precious, that the fruit found in them will be better than gold and precious stones, and that what she begets in souls has greater value than cherished silver, which signifies every kind of affection possible in this life.*[27]

Feminist thinkers and theologians are rediscovering John's wisdom writings which have great contributions to make in the fields of Christian and Jewish spirituality, especially in reference to the notions of *sophia* and *shekhinah* respectively. Constance FitzGerald points out the potential of rediscovering John's wisdom texts for spirituality today:

> *I have been working for a number of years with wisdom in John of the Cross. As I have searched and analyzed his many wisdom texts and tried to interface them with contemporary studies and the tradition of wisdom in Jewish theology and in the New Testament, I have discovered considerable potential for spirituality today.*[28]

For FitzGerald, the feminine image of God as divine wisdom is well treated in St. John of the Cross's writings. And from a feminist contemporary perspective, it is clear that John's depictions of Christ having been portrayed as divine wisdom are more in tune with primitive Christianity. Therefore, John offers us an alternative reading to the conventional theological image of Christ, which includes both masculine and feminine images of God. For instance, FitzGerald might have understood John's wisdom texts as a major contribution to solving contemporary Christological problems by stating:

> *This is where the tradition of Wisdom in mysticism, so long muted and marginalized but embodied with such prophetic power in John of the Cross's writings, will reassure us and enable theology to speak anew about Jesus Christ. The mysticism of John of the Cross supports a Sophia-God image, and a Sophia-God image, before everything else, subverts the*

---

[27] Ibid., 127; *Ascent* 1.4.8.

[28] Constance FitzGerald, "Transformation in Wisdom," in *Carmel and Contemplation*, 283.

way we understand God. It has the potential, therefore, to transform not only our consciousness and desire but most of all to change radically our theological discourse.[29]

John was well rooted in the eremitical-prophetic tradition following the Teresian reform which perfectly balances the contemplative life and the active life. In my opinion, Teresa's preference for the mixed life could easily explain why John left the Calced Carmelite Order, forgot his plans of joining the Carthusian Order, and became the coadjutor and religious reformer, together with Teresa, of the Discalced Carmelite tradition.

This study has demonstrated that St. John of the Cross was a contemplative in action within the parameters of his own monastic religious order. Although Panikkar's tripartite model owes its philosophical framework to the Hindu tradition, it is nonetheless an intellectual system that can be used by both Western and Eastern religious thinkers. I found Panikkar's typology very useful. I was able to focus on the Carmelite saint's threefold mystical paths to salvation. Indeed, St. John of the Cross was a mystic of action, wisdom, and devotion.

---

[29] Ibid., 342.

ACKNOWLEDGMENTS

I am grateful to the institute of Carmelite studies for permission to quote from the Kavanaugh-Rodriguez translation of the collected works of St. John of the Cross. I am especially appreciative to the editor of *Pacem in Terris* Press, Dr. Joe Holland for offering his helpful criticisms and suggestions over the past two years.

A special thanks to my colleagues in the philosophy and religious studies department for their continuous support that has allowed me over the years to do research on the Spanish mystics and Thomas Merton. It would be impossible to share my knowledge about St. John of the Cross without the faculty-development grants I have received during my tenure at Valdosta State University, after delivering numerous lectures at different conferences, spiritual centers, and monastic settings here in the United states and Abroad.

I cannot forget to mention the many opportunities that the International Thomas Merton society has offered me and countless of other Daggy and Shannon Scholars in their effort to support my intellectual and spiritual quest as a SanJuanist and as a Mertonian scholar.

My sincere thanks go to all who directly or indirectly have helped me in this laborious process going back to my undergraduate years at St. Thomas University (Miami Gardens, Florida), where I was fortunate to have great professors who encouraged me to follow my passion on the study of the mystics.

Later as a graduate student, I found the resources needed to be successful in my future life as an academician after studying philosophy at Boston College and after studying theology and religious studies at Boston University.

Moreover, I owe my deep thanks to the Discalced Carmelites in Spain, who assisted me with valuable information in my frequent visits to their monasteries, convents, and archives.

A special thanks to my family in Spain and in the United States for their full support all these years. Finally, I thank my wife Gabriela for her patience and for her dedicated attention to allow me to become the best version of who I am. Without all your love and full support, I would not be where I am today.

MONUMENTS & STATUES OF
JOHN OF THE CROSS & TERESA OF AVILA

Statue of Saint Teresa walking in Avila, Spain

Statue of Saint John in Úbeda, Spain

Monument of Saint Teresa in Avila, Spain

Statue in Spain of Saint John of the Cross Mystical Doctor

Memorial to Saint John of the Cross in Segovia, Spain

Painting in Spain of Teresa and Juan

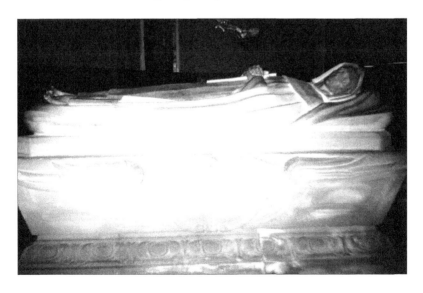

Tomb of Saint John in Úbeda, Spain

Statue of Saint Teresa in Avila, Spain

Monument of Saint John in La Carolina, Spain

Painting of Saint John & Saint Teresa in Spain

Monument to Saint John in Fontiveros, Spain

Painting of Saint John at the Hermitage of Peñuela, Spain

Wax figure of Saint John in Museum of Úbeda, Spain

Aqueduct constructed by Saint John in Granada, Spain

BIBLIOGRAPHY

Abellán, José Luis. "Místicos y ascetas en una España alucinada".

In *Mística y sociedad en diálogo. La experiencia interior y las normas de convivencia*. Edited by Francisco J. Sánchez Rodríguez. Madrid: Editorial Trotta, 2006.

Álvarez, Javier. *Mística y depresion: san Juan de la Cruz*. Madrid: Editorial Trotta, 1997.

Asín Palacios, Miguel. *Saint John of the Cross and Islam*. Translated by Howard W. Yoder and Elmer H. Douglas. New York: Vantage Press, 1981.

Astigarraga, Juan Luis, Agustí Borrell, and F. Javier Martín de Lucas, eds.*Concordancias de los Escritos de San Juan de la Cruz*. Roma: Teresianum, 1990.

Baralt, Luce López. *Asedios a lo Indecible: San Juan de la Cruz canta al éxtasis transformante*. Madrid: Editorial Trotta, 1998.

Barnstone, Willis. *The Poems of Saint John of the Cross*. New York: A New Directions Book, 1972.

Bernadicou, Paul J. "Contemporary Guides to John of the Cross." *Spiritual Life* 44:1 (1998): 4-5.

Brenan, Gerald. *The Literature of the Spanish People*: *From Roman Times to the Present*. NewYork: Meridian Books, 1967.

———. *St John of the Cross*: *His Life and Poetry*. Cambridge: Cambridge University Press, 1973.

Buber, Martin. *I and Thou*. New York: Macmillan Publishing, 1987.

Buggert, Donald W. "The Contemplative as Iconoclast." In *Carmel and Contemplation: Transforming Human Consciousness,* edited by Kevin Culligan and Regis Jordan, 62-63. Washington, District of Columbia: ICS Publications, 2000.

Campbell, Camille Anne. *Meditations with John of the Cross*. Santa Fe, New Mexico: Bear & Company, 1989.

Carabine, Deirdre. *The Unknown God. Negative Theology in the Platonic Tradition: Plato to Eriugena*. Louvain, Belgium: Peeters Press, 1995.

Casaldáliga, Pedro, and José María Vigil. *Political Holiness*. Maryknoll, New York: Orbis Books, 1994.

Cervantes, Miguel de. *Don Quixote*. Edited and translated by Henry E. Watts. London: Bernard Quaritch, 1888.

Chandler, Richard E., and Kessel Schwartz. *A New History of Spanish Literature*. Baton Rouge, Lousiana: Louisiana State University Press, 1991.

Crisógono de Jesús, Matías del Niño Jesús and Lucinio Ruano, eds. *Vida y Obras de San Juan de la Cruz*. Madrid: Biblioteca de Autores Cristianos, 1978.

Cócera, Katia. *San Juan de la Cruz y el yoga*. Madrid: Editorial de Espiritualidad, 2010.

Cummins, Norbert. *Freedom to Rejoice: Understanding St John of the Cross*. London: HarperCollinsReligious, 1991.

Daniel A. Dombrowski, *St. John of the Cross: An Appreciation*. New York: State University of New York Press, 1992.

De Tapia, Serafín. "Las huellas y el legado de las tres culturas religiosas en Ávila". In *Vivencia Mistica y Tejido Social*. Zamora: Ediciones Monte Casion, 2006: 179-227.

Dicken, E.W. Trueman. *The Crucible of Love: A Study of the Mysticism of St. Teresa of Jesus and St. John of the Cross*. New York: Sheed and Ward, 1963.

Doohan, Leonard. *The Contemporary Challenge of John of the Cross: An Introduction to His Life and Teaching*. Washington, District of Columbia: ICS Publications, 1995.

D'Souza, Rudolf V. *The BhagavadGita and St. John of the Cross: A Comparative Study of the Dynamism of Spiritual Growth in the Process of God-Realisation*. Roma: Editrice Pontificia Universita Gregoriana, 1996.

Dubay, Thomas. *Fire Within*: *St. Teresa of Avila, St. John of the Cross, and the Gospel--on Prayer*. San Francisco: Ignatius Press, 1989.

Dunn Mascetti, Manuela. *Christian Mysticism*. New York: Hyperion, 1998.

Dyckman, Katherine Marie, and L. Patrick Carroll. *Inviting the Mystic, Supporting the Prophet*: *An Introduction to Spiritual Direction*. New York: Paulist Press, 1981.

Egan, Harvey D. *An Anthology of Christian Mysticism*. Collegeville, Minnesota: The Liturgical Press, 1996.

Egan, Keith. "Dark Night," in *Carmel and Contemplation*: *Transforming Human Consciousness*, edited by Kevin Culligan and Regis Jordan, 244-245. Washington, District of Columbia: ICS Publications, 2000.

_____. "Thomas Merton's Approach to St. John of the Cross," in *The Merton Annual: Studies in Culture, Spirituality and Social Concerns* Volume 20, edited by Victor A. Kramer. Louisville: Fons Vitae, 2007.

Feldmeier, Peter. *Christianity Looks East: Comparing the Spiritualities of John of the Cross and Buddhaghosa*. New York: Paulist Press, 2006.

FitzGerald, Constance. "Transformation in Wisdom." In *Carmel and Contemplation*: *Transforming Human Consciousness*, edited by Kevin Culligan and Regis Jordan, 283. Washington, District of Columbia: ICS Publications, 2000.

_____. *Women's Spirituality*. New York: Paulist Press, 1986.

Flinders, Carol Lee. *Enduring Grace*. San Francisco: HarperSanFrancisco, 1993.

Frost, Bede *Saint John of the Cross. Doctor of Divine Love*: *An Introduction to His Philosophy, Theology and Spirituality*. London: Hodder & Stoughton, 1937.

Fülöp-Miller, René. *The Saints that Moved the World*. New York: Collier Books, 1962.

Gabriel of St. Mary Magdalen. *St. John of the Cross: Doctor of Divine Love and Contemplation*. Westminster, Maryland: The Newman Press, 1954.

Gaitán, José Damian. *Negación y plenitud en San Juan de la Cruz*. Madrid: Editorial de Espiritualidad, 1995.

Galilea, Segundo. *The Future of Our Past*: *The Spanish Mystics Speak to Contemporary Spirituality*. Notre Dame, Indiana: Ave Maria Press, 1985.

Garrido, Pablo María. *San Juan de la Cruz y Francisco de Yepes: En torno a la biografía de los dos hermanos*. Salamanca: Ediciones Sígueme, 1989.

Girón-Negrón, Luis M. "Dionysian Thought in Sixteenth-Century Spanish Mystical Theology." In *Modern Theology* Volume 24, Issue 4. 29 August 2008. https://doi.org/10.1111/j.1468-0025.2008.00494.x. Accessed April 1, 2018.

Gómez, Juan Enrique. "El árbol más viejo: San Juan de la Cruz escribía junto a él en el convento." *Ideal* 9 (October 1997): 12.

Gómez-Menor Fuentes, José. *El linaje familiar de santa Teresa y de san Juan de la Cruz: Sus parientes toledanos*. Toledo, Spain: Gráficas Cervantes, 1970.

Gutiérrez, Gustavo. *On Job*. Translated by Matthew J. O'Connell. Quezon City, Philippines: Claretian Publications, 1987.

_____. *We Drink from Our Own Wells*: *The Spiritual Journey of a People*. Translated by Matthew J. O'Connell. Maryknoll, New York: Orbis Books, 1984.

Happold, F.C. *Mysticism*: *A Study and An Anthology*. New York: Penguin Books, 1988.

Hardy, Richard P. *John of the Cross: Man and Mystic*. Boston: Pauline Books, 2004.

Hatzfeld, Helmut A. *Santa Teresa de Ávila*. New York: Twayne Publishers, 1969.

Herrera, R. A. *Silent Music: The Life, Work, and Thought of St. John of the Cross*. Grand Rapids, Michigan: William B. Eermans Publishing Company, 2004.

Hocking, William E. *The Meaning of God in Human Experience*: *A Philosophic Study of Religion*. New Haven, Connecticut: Yale University Press, 1955.

Hopkins, Jasper. *Nicholas of Cusa: On Learned Ignorance*. Minneapolis: The Arthur J. Banning Press, 1990.

James, William. *The Varieties of Religious Experience*. New York: Penguin Books, 1985.

John of the Cross. *The Collected Works of Saint John of the Cross*. Translated by Kieran Kavanaugh and Otilio Rodríguez. Washington, District of Columbia: ICS Publications, 1991.

Johnson, Elizabeth A. *Friends of God and Prophets*: *A Feminist Theological Reading of the Communion of Saints*. New York: Continuum, 1999.

Johnston, William. *The Inner Eye of Love: Mysticism and Religion*. San Francisco: Harper & Row, Publishers, 1982.

_____. *Mystical Theology*: *The Science of Love*. London: HarperCollins Publishers, 1995.

Kavanaugh, Kieran. "Saint John of the Cross." In *Welcome to Carmel: A Handbook for Aspirants to the Discalced Carmelite Secular Order*. Edited by Michael D. Griffin, 142-147. Hubertus, WI: Teresian Charism Press, 1998.

Kohn, Livia. *Early Chinese Mysticism: Philosophy and Soteriology in the Taoist Tradition*. Princeton, New Jersey: Princeton University Press, 1992.

Maccise, Camilo. "John of the Cross and the New Evangelization." *Spiritual Life* 38:3 (1992): 164.

María de la Cruz. "Proceso de Ubeda." In *Procesos de Beatificación y Canonización de San Juan de la Cruz,* Tomo V, edited by A. Fortes and F. J. Cuevas, 487. Burgos: Editorial Monte Carmelo, 1994.

Martínez González, Emilio J. *Tras las huellas de Juan de la Cruz: nueva biografía*. Madrid: Espiritualidad, 2006.

Matthew, Iain. *The Impact of God: Soundings from St John of the Cross*. London: Hodder & Stoughton, 1995.

McCutcheon, Caroline. "The Cross of a Friend." *Sufi: A Journal in Sufism* (Spring 1995): 11.

McDonnell, Thomas P. *Saints for All Seasons.* Edited by John J. Delaney. Garden City, New York: Image Books, 1978.

McGinn, Bernard. "The Role of the Carmelites in the History of Western Mysticism." In *Carmel and Contemplation*: *Transforming Human Consciousness,* edited by Kevin Culligan and Regis Jordan, 47. Washington, District of Columbia: ICS Publications, 2000.

Merton, Thomas. *The Ascent to Truth*. New York: A Harvest Book, 1981.

_____. *The Climate of Monastic Prayer*. Kalamazoo, Michigan: Cistercian Publications, 1969.

_____. *Conjectures of a Guilty Bystander*. New York: The Macmillan Company, 1967.

_____. *Contemplation in a World of Action*. Boston: Mandala Books, 1980.

_____. *Contemplation in a World of Action*. London: Unwin Paperbacks, 1980.

_____. *Contemplative Prayer*. New York: Image Books, 1990.

_____. *Disputed Questions*. New York: A Mentor-Omega Book, 1965.

_____. *Faith and Violence*. Notre Dame: University of Notre Dame Press, 1968.

_____. *The Literary Essays of Thomas Merton*. Edited by Patrick Hart. New York: New Directions, 1985.

_____. *The New Man*. New York: The Noonday Press, 1993.

_____. *On Saint Bernard*. Kalamazoo, Michigan: Cistercian Publication, 1980.

_____. *Seeds of Contemplation*. New York: A Dell Book, 1956.

_____. *Spiritual Direction & Meditation*. Collegeville, Minnesota: The Liturgical Press, 1960.

_____. *The Waters of Siloe*. New York: Image Books, 1962.

_____. *Zen and the Birds of Appetite*. New York: A New Directions Book, 1968.

Moore, John M. *Theories of Religious Experience: With Special Reference to James, Otto and Bergson*. New York: Round Table Press, 1938.

Moore, Thomas. *Dark Nights of the Soul: A Guide to Finding your Way through Life's Ordeals*. New York: Gotham Books, 2004.

Muñoz Iglesias, Salvador. *Lo Religioso en el Quijote*. Toledo: Estudio teológico de S. Ildefonso, 1989.

Muto, Susan. *Words of Wisdom for our World: The Precautions and Counsels of St. John of the Cross*. Washington, D.C.: ICS Publications, 1996.

Nasr, S.H. *The Need for a Sacred Science*. Albany, New York: State University of New York Press, 1993.

Neville, Robert. *Soldier, Sage, Saint*. New York: Fordham University Press, 1978.

Pacho, Eulogio. *S. Juan de la Cruz. Obras Completas*. Burgos: Monte Carmelo, 1993.

Panikkar, Raimundo. *The Cosmotheandric Experience: Emerging Religious Consciousness*. Maryknoll, New York: Orbis Books, 1993.

———. *A Dwelling Place for Wisdom*. Louisville, Kentucky: Westminster/John Knox Press, 1993.

———. *La Experiencia de Dios*. Madrid: PPC, 1994.

———. *La Trinidad y la Experiencia Religiosa*. Barcelona: Ediciones Obelisco, 1989.

———. *Worship and Secular Man*. Maryknoll, New York: Orbis Books, 1973.

Peers, E. Allison. *Spirit of Flame: A Study of St. John of the Cross*. New York: Morehouse-Gorham, 1945.

———. *Studies of the Spanish Mystics*. London: The Sheldon Press, 1927.

Perrin, David B. "Foundations for a Hermeneutical Interpretation of the *Cántico Espiritual* of Juan de la Cruz." *Science et Esprit* 48:1 (1996): 76.

Poveda Piérola, Lola. *Conciencia energía y pensar místico: El hoy de Teresa de Jesus y Juan de la Cruz*. Bilbao: Desclee de Brouwer, 2011.

Rodríguez, José Vicente. *Florecillas de San Juan de la Cruz: La hondura de lo humano*. Madrid: Ediciones Paulinas, 1990.

Ruffing, Janet K. "Ignatian Mysticism of Service." In *Mysticism & Social Transformation*, edited by Janet K. Ruffing, 107. Syracuse, New York: Syracuse University Press, 2001.

Sánchez Lora, Jose Luis. *San Juan de la Cruz en la Revolución Copernicana*. Madrid: Editorial de Espiritualidad, 1992.

Serrán-Pagán, Cristóbal. "Divine Mercy in Thomas Merton and St. John of the Cross: Encountering the Dark Nights in the Human Soul." In *The Merton Annual: Studies in Culture, Spirituality and Social Concerns* Volume 30, edited by Deborah Pope Kehoe and Joseph Quinn Raab, 117-130. Louisville: Fons Vitae, 2017.

_____. "Merton's Understanding of the Mystical Doctrine of Saint John of the Cross's Dark Night of the Soul." In *Thomas Merton: A Mind Awake in the Dark*. Edited by Paul M. Pearson, Danny Sullivan and Ian Thomson, 165-173. Abergavenny, UK: Three Peaks Press, 2002.

_____. "Seeds of Hope in Times of Crisis: Saint John of the Cross and Thomas Merton." In *Seeds of Hope: Thomas Merton's Contemplative Message*. Edited by Fernando Beltrán Llavador and Paul M. Pearson, 81-100. Zamora: Ediciones Monte Casino, 2008.

Siddheswarananda, Swami. *Hindu Thought and Carmelite Mysticism*. Translated by William Buchanan. Delhi: Motilal Banarsidass Publishers, 1998.

Silverio de Santa Teresa. *Historia del Carmen Descalzo en España, Portugal y América*. Burgos: El Monte Carmelo, 1936.

The Sisters of Notre Dame, *Life of Saint John of the Cross: Mystical Doctor*. New York: Benziger Brothers, 1927.

Slattery, Peter. *The Springs of Carmel: An Introduction to Carmelite Spirituality*. New York: Alba House, 1991.

Stace, W.T. *Mysticism and Philosophy*. Los Angeles: Jeremy P. Tarcher, 1960.

Steggink, Otger, and Efrén de la Madre de Dios. *Tiempo y Vida de San Juan de la Cruz*. Madrid: Biblioteca de Autores Cristianos, 1992.

Teasdale, Wayne. *The Mystic Heart: Discovering a Universal Spirituality in the World's Religions*. Novato, California: New World Library, 1999.

Teresa of Avila. *The Collected Works of St. Teresa of Avila*. Edited by Kieran Kavanaugh and Otilio Rodríguez. Washington, District of Columbia: ICS Publications, 1980.

Thompson, Colin. "Saint John of the Cross." *Oxford Bibliographies*. 31 August 2015. www.oxfordbibliographies.com. Accessed April 23, 2018.

Underhill, Evelyn. *Mysticism*. New York: The New American Library, 1974.

Welch, John. *An Introduction to John of the Cross: When Gods Die*. New York: Paulist Press, 1990.

Zimmerman, Benedict. "The Development of Mysticism in the Carmelite Order." In *The Ascent of Mount Carmel,* edited and translated by David Lewis, 3. London: Thomas Baker, 1928.

OTHER BOOKS
FROM PACEM IN TERRIS PRESS

BRETTON WOODS INSTITUTIONS & NEOLIBERALISM
Historical Critique of Policies, Structures, & Governance of the International Monetary Fund
& the World Bank, with Case Studies
Mark Wolff

THE WHOLE STORY:
The Wedding of Science & Religion
Norman Carroll, 2018

PADRE MIGUEL
A Memoir of My Catholic Missionary Experience in Bolivia
amidst Postcolonial Transformation of Church and State
Michael J. Gillgannon, 2018

POSTMODERN ECOLOGICAL SPIRITUALITY
Catholic-Christian Hope for the Dawn of a Postmodern Ecological Civilization Rising
from within the Spiritual Dark Night of Modern Industrial Civilization
Joe Holland, 2017

JOURNEYS TO RENEWED CONSECRATION
Religious Life after Fifty Years of Vatican II
Emeka Obiezu, OSA & John Szura, OSA, Editors, 2017

THE CRUEL ELEVENTH-CENTURY IMPOSITION OF
WESTERN CLERICAL CELIBACY
A Monastic-Inspired Attack on Catholic Episcopal & Clerical Families
Joe Holland, 2017

LIGHT, TRUTH, & NATURE
Practical Reflections on Vedic Wisdom & Heart-Centered Meditation
In Seeking a Spiritual Basis for Nature, Science, Evolution, & Ourselves
Thomas Pliske, 2017

THOMAS BERRY IN ITALY
Reflections on Spirituality & Sustainability
Elisabeth M. Ferrero, Editor, 2016

PETER MAURIN'S
ECOLOGICAL LAY NEW MONASTICISM
*A Catholic Green Revolution Developing
Rural Ecovillages, Urban Houses of Hospitality,
& Eco-Universities for a New Civilization*
Joe Holland, 2015

PROTECTION OF RELIGIOUS MINORITIES
*A Symposium Organized by Pax Romana at the United Nations
and the United Nations Alliance of Civilizations*
Dean Elizabeth F. Defeis & Peter F. O'Connor, Editors, 2015

BOTTOM ELEPHANTS
*Catholic Sexual Ethics & Pastoral Practice in Africa:
The Challenge of Women Living within Patriarchy
& Threatened by HIV-Positive Husbands*
Daniel Ude Asue, 2014

CATHOLIC LABOR PRIESTS
*Five Giants in the United States Catholic Bishops Social Action Department
Volume I of US Labor Priests During the 20th Century*
Patrick Sullivan, 2014

CATHOLIC SOCIAL TEACHING & UNIONS
IN CATHOLIC PRIMARY & SECONDARY SCHOOLS
The Clash between Theory & Practice within the United States
Walter "Bob" Baker, 2014

SPIRITUAL PATHS TO
A GLOBAL & ECOLOGICAL CIVILIZATION
Reading the Signs of the Times with Buddhists, Christians, & Muslims
John Raymaker & Gerald Grudzen, with Joe Holland, 2013

PACEM IN TERRIS
*Its Continuing Relevance for the Twenty-First Century
(Papers from the 50th Anniversary Conference at the United Nations)*
Josef Klee & Francis Dubois, Editors, 2013

PACEM IN TERRIS
*Summary & Commentary for the Famous Encyclical Letter
of Pope John XXIII on World Peace*
Joe Holland, 2012

100 YEARS OF CATHOLIC SOCIAL TEACHING
DEFENDING WORKERS & THEIR UNIONS
Summaries & Commentaries for Five Landmark Papal Encyclicals
Joe Holland, 2012

HUMANITY'S AFRICAN ROOTS
Remembering the Ancestors' Wisdom
Joe Holland, 2012

THE "POISONED SPRING" OF ECONOMIC LIBERTARIANISM
*Menger, Mises, Hayek, Rothbard: A Critique from
Catholic Social Teaching of the Austrian School of Economics*
Pax Romana / Cmica-usa
Angus Sibley, 2011

BEYOND THE DEATH PENALTY
The Development in Catholic Social Teaching
Florida Council of Catholic Scholarship
D. Michael McCarron & Joe Holland, Editors, 2007

THE NEW DIALOGUE OF CIVILIZATIONS
*A Contribution from Pax Romana
International Catholic Movement for Intellectual & Cultural Affairs*
Pax Romana / Cmica-usa
Roza Pati & Joe Holland, Editors, 2002

---

*This book and other books from Pacem in Terris Press,
are available at:*

www.amazon.com/books

CPSIA information can be obtained
at www.ICGtesting.com
Printed in the USA
BVHW041146190419
546012BV00011B/99/P